400 Vodka Based Cocktails

Lev Well

Copyright © 2015

All rights reserved.

ISBN: **1515367991**
ISBN-13: **978-1515367994**

Disclaimer

All recipes are used at the discretion of the consumer. We cannot be responsible for any hazards, loss or damage that may occur as a result of any recipe used.

For those with special needs, allergies, requirements or health problems, in the event of any doubt, please contact your medical adviser prior to the use of any recipe.

CONTENTS

Absolut Anti-freeze #2 recipe 24

Absolut Anti-freeze recipe 24

Absolut Dream recipe 25

Absolut Evergreen recipe 25

Absolut Hulk recipe 25

Absolut Lemonade recipe 26

Absolut Limousine recipe 26

Absolut Mixer recipe 27

Absolut Motherfucker recipe 27

Absolut Redhead recipe 28

Absolut Royal Fuck recipe 28

Absolut Salty Dog recipe 29

Absolut Sex recipe 29

Absolut Sexy Lemonade Punch recipe 30

Absolut Splash recipe 31

Absolut Stress #2 recipe 31

Absolut Stress recipe 31

Absolut Tooch recipe 32

Absolute Monster recipe 33

Absolute Suicide recipe 33

Absolutely Fruity recipe 34

Absolutly Screwed recipe 34

Absolutly Screwed Up recipe 34

Adam Bomb recipe 35

Afterburner #2 recipe 36

Aladdin Sane recipe 36

Alcoholic Sherbert Delight recipe 37

Alebrije recipe 37

Alien Secretion #2 recipe 38

Almost Heaven recipe 38

Alzheimers recipe 39

Apeachy Procaccini recipe 39

Apple Fucker recipe 40

Apple Martini recipe 40

Arizona Stingers recipe 41

Arizona Twister recipe 41

Astral Gateway recipe 42

AT&T recipe 43

Awesome Chandler recipe 43

B.F.D. recipe 44

Back Shot recipe 44

Backseat Boogie #2 recipe 45

Bald Pussy recipe 45

Ball of Fun recipe 46

Baltic Murder Mystery recipe 46

Barbie Shot recipe 47

Berry Fusion Martini recipe 47

Big Dumb Russian recipe 48

Bionic Beaver recipe 48

Bird Bomb recipe 49

Bizonkadonk Martini recipe 50

Black Martini #2 recipe 50

Black Orgasm recipe 51

Black Swedish Virgin recipe 51

Black Widow recipe 52

Blackberry Lane recipe 52

Blame It On Rio recipe 53

Blue Chili recipe 53

Blue Cosmopolitan recipe 54

Blue Dragon recipe 54

Blue Dragonfly recipe 55

Blue Grapes recipe 55

Blue Haze recipe 56

Blue MotherFucker recipe 56

Blue Screw recipe 57

Blue Slammer recipe 57

Blue Solute recipe 58

Bold Gold Monkey recipe 58

Boom Shaka Laka recipe 59

Brain Damage recipe 59

Bronx Martini recipe 59

Burberry Bulldog recipe 60

Buzz Lightyear recipe 61

Cabin Cooler recipe 61

Cactus Cooler recipe 62

California Gold Rush recipe 62

California Lemonade recipe 63

Canteloupe Dizzy recipe 63

Caribbean Ice Tea recipe 64

Caucasian recipe 64

Chambord Royale recipe 65

Charlie Coke recipe 65

Cherry Bomb #2 recipe 66

Cherry Lemon Drop recipe 66

Cherry Lover recipe 67

Chocolate Cake Shooter recipe 67

Chocolate Martini Lite recipe 68

Chocolate Orange recipe 68

Citron My Face recipe 69

Citron Splash Martini recipe 69

Citronade recipe 70

Coast-Line recipe 70

Cold Blood recipe 71

Cooter Cork recipe 71

Cosmo Katie recipe 72

Cosmo Kurant recipe 73

Cosmobellini recipe 73

Cosmopolitan Cocktail #2 recipe 74

Cosmopolitan Cocktail #4 recipe 74

Cossak recipe 75

Country Time recipe 75

Cowboy Killer recipe 76

Crantini recipe 76

Creamsicle #4 recipe 77

Crimson Tide recipe 77

Crooked Monkey recipe 78

Cruz Azul recipe 78

Cry Baby Blues recipe 79

Cucaracha #2 recipe 79

Cum Scorcher recipe 80

Currant Fuzzy Navel recipe 80

D & D Lay recipe 81

Dea Lea recipe 81

Deep Blue recipe 82

Dephaekt recipe 82

Dib Dab recipe 83

Dick Hard recipe 83

Dignified Iced Tea recipe 84

Diva recipe 84

Doggystyle recipe 85

Don Roberto recipe 85

Donna Reed recipe 86

Double Fudge Martini #2 recipe 86

Dry Lemonade recipe 87

Eagle Eye recipe 87

Ejhazz recipe 88

Electric Lemonade recipe 88

En Sann En recipe 89

Enigma recipe 89

Epidural recipe 90

Erictini recipe 90

Esirnus recipe 91

Espresso Martini recipe 92

Estonian Forest-Fire recipe 92

Evil Corona recipe 93

Fahrenheit 5000 recipe 93

Federal Law recipe 93

Feel This recipe 94

Flaming Jesus recipe 95

Flaming Lemon Drop recipe 95

Flaming Lemon recipe 96

Foreplay on the Neutral Ground recipe 96

Forest Funk recipe 97

Fox Poison recipe 97

Fraustadt recipe 98

French Cosmopolitan recipe 98

French Flamingo recipe 99

French Sailor recipe 99

Fruity Screaming Fuzzy Navel recipe 100

Fucking Hot recipe 100

Funky Cold Medina recipe 101

Funky Filly recipe 101

Funnel Cloud recipe 102

Fuquay Friday Night recipe 102

Fuzzy Ass recipe 103

Fuzzy Balls recipe 103

Fuzzy Martini recipe 104

Fuzzy Nuts recipe 104

G Bomb recipe 105

Gailwarning recipe 105

Get Faced recipe 106

Getaway Car recipe 106

Geting recipe 107

Gingervitas recipe 107

Girasole Cocktail recipe 108

Gold Wizard recipe 108

Good Fortune recipe 109

Grand Hawaiian Screw recipe 109

Grape Ape #2 recipe 109

Green Cow #2 recipe 110

Green Creeper recipe 110

Green Delight recipe 111

Green Froggy recipe 111

Green Slime recipe 112

Greven recipe 112

Grown-up Lemonade recipe 113

G-Spot Martini recipe 113

Gun Barrel recipe 114

H2O Martini recipe 114

Haleakala Martini recipe 115

Halfway Special recipe 115

Hand Job recipe 116

Hard Green Bricaki recipe 116

Harlem World Seven recipe 117

Hawaiian Volcano recipe 117

Hematoma recipe 118

Honey Bunny recipe 118

Hot Tub recipe 119

Hurlyburly recipe 120

Ice House Highball recipe 120

Idaho Dimetapp recipe 121

Inferno recipe 121

Intercourse recipe 122

Inverted Pyramid Martini recipe 122

Inverted Traffic Light recipe 123

Italian Ice #2 recipe 123

Italian Stallion #2 recipe 124

Jacobs Haze recipe 124

Jersey Shore Cherry Lemonade recipe 125

Joe Cassano recipe 125

Jogeir recipe 126

John Daly recipe 126

John Rocker recipe 127

Johnny Bravo recipe 127

Johnny Rev recipe 128

Joy Ride recipe 128

Juicy Guiness Premier recipe 129

Kamakazie #2 recipe 129

Krypto Kami recipe 130

Kurant Collins recipe 130

Kurant recipe 131

Kurant Shot recipe 131

Kurant Tea recipe 132

Lake George Iced Tea recipe 132

Lakeside Lemonade recipe 133

Lava Lamp recipe 133

Lemon Drop #2 recipe 134

Lemon Drop #3 recipe 134

Lemon Drop #5 recipe 135

Lemon Drop #6 recipe 135

Lemon Drop Martini #2 recipe 136

Lemon Joe recipe 137

Lemon Shot recipe 137

Lemon Twist recipe 138

Lemon Twister recipe 138

Lemonade Bomb recipe 139

Lick and a Promise recipe 139

Liquid Cocaine #2 recipe 140

Liquid Desert recipe 140

Long Iver Iced Tea recipe 141

Loopy Lemonade recipe 141

Love Potion recipe 142

Lucky Double recipe 142

Ludvika Walker recipe 143

Lyndy recipe 143

M.V.P. recipe 144

Magic Mountain Dew recipe 144

Magic Punch recipe 145

Malibu Paradise recipe 145

Malibu Smash recipe 146

Mandarin Crush recipe 146

Mandarin Delight recipe 147

Mandarin Dream recipe 147

Mandarin Split recipe 148

Mandarin Sunrise recipe 148

Mandrin Cherry Smash recipe 149

Maria-Rocker recipe 149

Martina Mandarina recipe 150

Martini Dominikanis recipe 150

Mazerati recipe 151

Mean Green Machine recipe 151

Melon Martini recipe 152

Meloncholy Baby recipe 152

Merry Christmas recipe 153

Metropolitan #2 recipe 153

Miami Hurricane recipe 154

Midori Hack recipe 154

Miss Pastore recipe 155

Missle Pop recipe 155

Mogadon recipe 156

Moilanen recipe 156

Mona-Lisa recipe 157

Mongolian Motherfucker recipe 157

Naked Navel recipe 158

Nestle recipe 158

New York Lemonade recipe 159

Nickel Alloy recipe 159

Nickel recipe 160

Nicolalas recipe 160

Northern Lights recipe 161

Nuclear Slush recipe 161

Nuclear Waste #2 recipe 162

Nurse recipe 162

NyQuil recipe 163

Orange Lion recipe 163

Orange Smasha recipe 164

Pajama Jackhammer recipe 164

Party Boy recipe 165

Party Girl recipe 165

Peachy Screw recipe 166

Peekaboo recipe 167

Pelvic Crusher recipe 167

Phantom recipe 167

Photon Torpedo recipe 168

Phreaker Cocktail recipe 168

Pimp Cocktail recipe 169

Pimp Punch recipe 169

Pine Needle recipe 170

Pineapple Snap recipe 170

Pink Clyt recipe 171

Pink Lemonade recipe 171

Pink Millenium recipe 172

Pink Panther #2 recipe 172

Pink Penocha recipe 173

Pink Pitch recipe 173

Pocima recipe 174

Poison Apple recipe 174

Porch Climber recipe 175

Postman recipe 175

Pure Pleasure recipe 176

Purple Fantasy recipe 176

Purple Love recipe 177

Purple Mexican recipe 177

Purple People Eater recipe 178

Purple Stealth recipe 178

Ragnar #3 recipe 179

Ragnar recipe 179

Red Eisentrout recipe 180

Red Manhattan recipe 180

Red Rock recipe 181

Reggae Ambassador recipe 181

Richie 50 recipe 182

Rising Skirt recipe 182

Roffsing recipe 183

Rumka recipe 183

Russian Sarin recipe 184

Sabra recipe 184

Salt and Pepper Martini recipe 185

San Diego Silver Bullet recipe 185

Scarlet Fever recipe 186

Schnapp It Up recipe 186

Scotty Boy recipe 186

Screwed Driver recipe 187

Scrumdriver recipe 187

Seizure recipe 188

Serena recipe 188

Sex On An Arizona Beach recipe 189

Sex on the Beach #4 recipe 189

Sex On The Beach #6 recipe 190

Sex on the Brain recipe 191

Sexual Trance recipe 191

Shark Attack recipe 192

Shetty Classic recipe 192

Skittle recipe 193

Skylab Fallout recipe 193

Slemmig Slyna recipe 194

Slippery Box recipe 194

Smoked Martini recipe 195

Smurf Piss #2 recipe 195

Snowshot recipe 196

South Beach Martini recipe 196

Southern Blast recipe 197

Southern Peach recipe 198

Spice and Ice recipe 198

Spooky Juice recipe 199

Sprawling Dubinsky recipe 199

Springtime recipe 200

Stardust recipe 200

Start Me Up recipe 201

Strap-O-Nilla Juice recipe 201

Sunflower Highball recipe 202

Sunset Breeze recipe 202

Suntory Cocktail recipe 203

Swedish Blue recipe 203

Swedish Polar Bear recipe 204

Swedish Polar Bear recipe 204

Tanga recipe 205

Taste of Winter recipe 205

Tattooed Love Goddess recipe 205

Texas Pink Cloud recipe 206

The Abba recipe 207

The Betty Ford recipe 207

The Bozek recipe 208

The BV recipe 208

The Cherry Bomb recipe 209

The Fuzzy Magnum recipe 209

The Hollywood recipe 210

The Lowee recipe 210

The Lunchbox recipe 210

The Triple recipe 211

Thirsty Marine recipe 212

Three Wise Men #3 recipe 212

Thunder King recipe 213

Thunder Peel recipe 213

Tie Me To The Bedpost - Hawaiian recipe 213

Tie Me To The Bedpost   Baby recipe 214

Tight Snatch recipe 215

Tom Collins ala Olsen recipe 215

Touchdown recipe 216

Triple Asp recipe 216

Triple Threat recipe 217

Tropical Binalada recipe 217

Tropical Hooter recipe 218

Tropical Life Saver #2 recipe 218

Tropical Lust recipe 219

Tropical Orgasm #3 recipe 219

Tropical Orgasm recipe 220

Tropical Storm Jack recipe 220

Troutie recipe 221

Under Current recipe 221

Under Kurant recipe 222

Vegas Lemon Drop Martini recipe 222

Very Berry Tonic recipe 223

Vicious Kiss recipe 223

Vodka Orange recipe 224

Vodka Passion recipe 224

Waverunner recipe 225

Widow Maker recipe 225

Wiper Fluid recipe 226

Wobbler recipe 226

Y2K Shot #2 recipe 227

Yaka recipe 227

Zadarade recipe 228

Zool recipe 228

Absolut Anti-freeze #2 recipe

Description
A delicious recipe for Absolut Anti-freeze #2, with Absolut® vodka, orange juice, DeKuyper® Peachtree schnapps, Midori® melon liqueur and creme de bananes.

Ingredients
4 oz Absolut® vodka
4 oz orange juice
1 oz DeKuyper® Peachtree schnapps
1 oz Midori® melon liqueur
1 dash creme de bananes

Instructions
Pour all ingredients into a cocktail shaker half-filled with ice cubes. Shake well, strain into a highball glass 3/4 filled with ice cubes, and serve.

Serving
Highball Glass

****

Absolut Anti-freeze recipe

Description
A delicious recipe for Absolut Anti-freeze, with Midori® melon liqueur, Absolut® Citron vodka, Sprite® soda and ice cubes.

Ingredients
1 part Midori® melon liqueur
2 parts Absolut® Citron vodka
2 parts Sprite® soda
ice cubes

Instructions
Pour ingredients over ice and strain into shot glasses.

Serving
Shot Glass

****

Absolut Dream recipe

Description
A delicious recipe for Absolut Dream, with Absolut® Mandrin vodka, sweet and sour mix and Chambord® raspberry liqueur.

Ingredients
1 1/2 oz Absolut® Mandrin vodka
1 oz sweet and sour mix
1/2 oz Chambord® raspberry liqueur

Instructions
Pour Absolut Mandrin into a cocktail/martini shaker. Add sweet and sour mix, and Chambord raspberry liqueur. Rim a cocktail glass with sugar. Shake and strain the contents of the cocktail shaker into the cocktail glass. Garnish with a twist of orange, and serve.

Serving
Cocktail Glass
****

Absolut Evergreen recipe

Description
A delicious recipe for Absolut Evergreen, with Absolut® Citron vodka, Pisang Ambon® liqueur and bitter lemon soda.

Ingredients
2/3 part Absolut® Citron vodka
1/3 part Pisang Ambon® liqueur
fill with bitter lemon soda

Instructions
Mix, pour over ice and top with bitter lemon.

Serving
Whiskey Sour Glass
****

Absolut Hulk recipe

Description
A delicious recipe for Absolut Hulk, with Absolut® Vanilia vodka, Midori® melon liqueur, gomme syrup, pineapple juice and lime juice.

Ingredients
2 1/2 oz Absolut® Vanilia vodka
2 1/2 oz Midori® melon liqueur
1/2 oz gomme syrup
3 1/2 oz pineapple juice
1 1/2 oz fresh lime juice

Instructions
Combine all ingredients in a cocktail shaker half-filled with ice cubes. Shake well, and strain into a collins glass 3/4 filled with ice cubes. Garnish with two pineapple leaves, and serve.

Serving
Collins Glass
****

Absolut Lemonade recipe

Description
A delicious recipe for Absolut Lemonade, with Absolut® Citron vodka, amaretto almond liqueur, sweet and sour mix, ice and Sprite® soda.

Ingredients
1 oz Absolut® Citron vodka
1 oz amaretto almond liqueur
2 oz sweet and sour mix
ice
Sprite® soda

Instructions
Mix alcohol, sweet and sour. Add Ice and top off with Sprite.

Serving
Collins Glass
****

Absolut Limousine recipe

Description
A delicious recipe for Absolut Limousine, with Absolut® Citron vodka, lime juice, ice and tonic water.

Ingredients
2 oz Absolut® Citron vodka
1 oz lime juice
ice
fill with tonic water

Instructions
Fill Absolut into a glass. Add Lime juice. Add Ice and lime wedges.

Serving
Highball Glass
****

Absolut Mixer recipe

Description
A delicious recipe for Absolut Mixer, with Absolut® Citron vodka, Absolut® Peppar vodka, Absolut® Kurant vodka, Absolut® vodka and orange juice.

Ingredients
1 oz Absolut® Citron vodka
1 oz Absolut® Peppar vodka
1 oz Absolut® Kurant vodka
1 oz Absolut® vodka
fill with orange juice

Instructions
Shake together over ice, and strain into a highball glass. Garnish with a lime wedge and a cherry.

Serving
Highball Glass
****

Absolut Motherfucker recipe

Description
A delicious recipe for Absolut Motherfucker, with Absolut® Citron vodka, Crown Royal® Canadian whisky, peach schnapps, triple sec, orange juice and pineapple juice.

Ingredients
1 1/2 oz Absolut® Citron vodka
1 1/2 oz Crown Royal® Canadian whisky
1 1/2 oz peach schnapps
1 1/2 oz triple sec
1 splash orange juice
1 splash pineapple juice

Instructions
Combine all ingredients in a cocktail shaker with ice. Shake vigorously as to form ice shavings and foam, pour entire contents into a highball glass and serve.

Serving
Highball Glass
****

Absolut Redhead recipe

Description
A delicious recipe for Absolut Redhead, with Absolut® Peppar vodka, grenadine syrup and limes.

Ingredients
1 oz Absolut® Peppar vodka
1 dash grenadine syrup
juice of 1/2 limes

Instructions
Shake with ice and strain into a rocks glass.

Serving
Old-Fashioned Glass
****

Absolut Royal Fuck recipe

Description
A delicious recipe for Absolut Royal Fuck, with Crown Royal® Canadian whisky, Absolut® Kurant vodka, peach schnapps, cranberry juice and pineapple juice.

Ingredients
1 oz Crown Royal® Canadian whisky
1/2 oz Absolut® Kurant vodka
1/2 oz peach schnapps
1 splash cranberry juice
1 splash pineapple juice

Instructions
Chill in tumbler, shake, and serve up in a rocks glass.

Serving
Old-Fashioned Glass
****

Absolut Salty Dog recipe

Description
A delicious recipe for Absolut Salty Dog, with Absolut® Peppar vodka and grapefruit juice.

Ingredients
1 1/2 oz Absolut® Peppar vodka
grapefruit juice

Instructions
Build in a salt rimmed highball glass and fill with grapefruit juice.

Serving
Highball Glass
****

Absolut Sex recipe

Description
A delicious recipe for Absolut Sex, with Absolut® Kurant vodka, Midori® melon liqueur, cranberry juice and Sprite® soda.

Ingredients
3/4 oz Absolut® Kurant vodka
3/4 oz Midori® melon liqueur
1 oz cranberry juice
1 splash Sprite® soda

Instructions
Shake Absolut Kurant, Midori, and Cranberry juice in shaker with ice.

Strain into a rocks glass with a splash of seven on top.

Serving
Old-Fashioned Glass
****

Absolut Sexy Lemonade Punch recipe

Description
A delicious recipe for Absolut Sexy Lemonade Punch, with Absolut® vodka, triple sec, 7-Up® soda, lemon juice, lemon, sweet and sour mix, sugar and grenadine syrup.

Ingredients
15 oz Absolut® vodka
7 1/2 oz triple sec
7 oz 7-Up® soda
4 oz lemon juice
1 lemon
sweet and sour mix
1/2 - 1 cup sugar
1/8 oz grenadine syrup

Instructions
Pour vodka, triple sec, 7-up, and lemon juice into a 64 ounce container. Slice a lemon, add, then almost-fill with sweet and sour mix. Add sugar and a touch of grenadine, and shake well. Serve into highball glasses. Stir or shake well with each serving to circulate the sugar.

Serving

Highball Glass
****

Absolut Splash recipe

Description
A delicious recipe for Absolut Splash, with Absolut® vodka and V8® vegetable juice.

Ingredients
1 1/2 oz Absolut® vodka
1 1/2 cups V8® vegetable juice

Instructions
Mix in a highball glass.

Serving
Highball Glass
****

Absolut Stress #2 recipe

Description
A delicious recipe for Absolut Stress #2, with Absolut® vodka, peach schnapps, coconut liqueur, cranberry juice and pineapple juice.

Ingredients
1 1/2 oz Absolut® vodka
1/2 oz peach schnapps
1/2 oz coconut liqueur
1 1/2 oz cranberry juice
1 1/2 oz pineapple juice

Instructions
Mix well. Garnish with a slice of orange and a cherry, and serve.

****

Absolut Stress recipe

Description
A delicious recipe for Absolut Stress, with Absolut® vodka, Malibu® coconut rum, peach schnapps, orange juice, pineapple juice and cranberry juice.

Ingredients
1/2 oz Absolut® vodka
1/2 oz Malibu® coconut rum
1/2 oz peach schnapps
1 oz orange juice
1 oz pineapple juice
1 oz cranberry juice

Instructions
Pour all ingredients into a mixing tin and shake with ice. Pour into a collins glass. No garnish.

Serving
Collins Glass
****

Absolut Tooch recipe

Description
A delicious recipe for Absolut Tooch, with Absolut® vodka, Southern Comfort® peach liqueur, tequila, Chambord® raspberry liqueur, triple sec, pineapple juice and cranberry juice.

Ingredients
1 oz Absolut® vodka
1 oz Southern Comfort® peach liqueur
1 oz tequila
1 oz Chambord® raspberry liqueur
1 oz triple sec
1 1/2 oz pineapple juice
1 1/2 oz cranberry juice

Instructions
Chill with ice and strain into shot glasses.

Serving
Shot Glass
****

Absolute Monster recipe

Description
A delicious recipe for Absolute Monster, with Absolut® vanilla vodka, Monster® energy drink and ice cubes.

Ingredients
4 oz Absolut® vanilla vodka
4 oz Monster® energy drink
4 oz ice cubes

Instructions
Combine the Absolut vanilla vodka, Monster energy drink and ice cubes in a blender. Blend until slushy, pour into a highball glass, and serve.

Serving
Highball Glass
****

Absolute Suicide recipe

Description
A delicious recipe for Absolute Suicide, with DeKuyper® Sour Apple Pucker schnapps, DeKuyper® Watermelon Pucker schnapps, DeKuyper Island Blue Pucker and Absolut® vodka.

Ingredients
1/4 oz DeKuyper® Sour Apple Pucker schnapps
1/4 oz DeKuyper® Watermelon Pucker schnapps
1/4 oz DeKuyper Island Blue Pucker
1/4 oz Absolut® vodka

Instructions
Chill each ingredient. Pour into a shot glass in equal parts, and serve.

Serving

Shot Glass
****

Absolutely Fruity recipe

Description
A delicious recipe for Absolutely Fruity, with banana liqueur, watermelon liqueur and Absolut® vodka.

Ingredients
1/2 oz banana liqueur
1/2 oz watermelon liqueur
1/2 oz Absolut® vodka

Instructions
Mix banana and watermelon liqueur in shot glass top with vodka.

Serving
Shot Glass
****

Absolutly Screwed recipe

Description
A delicious recipe for Absolutly Screwed, with Absolut® Mandrin vodka and orange juice.

Ingredients
1/2 oz Absolut® Mandrin vodka
1/2 oz orange juice

Instructions
Mix OJ and Mandrin then enjoy.

Serving
Shot Glass
****

Absolutly Screwed Up recipe

Description
A delicious recipe for Absolutly Screwed Up, with Absolut® Citron vodka, orange juice, triple sec and ginger ale.

Ingredients
1 shot Absolut® Citron vodka
1 shot orange juice
1 shot triple sec
fill with ginger ale

Instructions
Shake it up it tasts better that way, but you can stir it if you want. 6 of those and you will be wasted for the rest of the night.

Serving
Collins Glass
****

Adam Bomb recipe

Description
A delicious recipe for Adam Bomb, with Jose Cuervo® Especial gold tequila, Absolut® vodka, Bacardi® white rum, triple sec, fruits, ice, sugar and fruit juice.

Ingredients
1 part Jose Cuervo® Especial gold tequila
1 part Absolut® vodka
1 part Bacardi® white rum
1/2 part triple sec
fruits
1/2 glass ice
sugar
2 pints fruit juice

Instructions
1. Add ice to a blender (or to a glass if you prefer on the rocks).

2. Add the fruit and fruit juice depending on personal preference, then add the rum, vodka, tequila, and triple sec. Blend until smooth.

3. Rim a glass with sugar or salt and pour in the mixture. Garnish with a lemon or lime slice.

Serving
Margarita Glass
****

Afterburner #2 recipe

Description
A delicious recipe for Afterburner #2, with Absolut® vodka and Tabasco® sauce.

Ingredients
1 oz Absolut® vodka
1/2 oz Tabasco® sauce

Instructions
Pour 1 shot a vodka pour 1/2 shot of Tobasco sauce in seperate shot glass. (take vodka shot immediately followed by the Tobasco shot)

***amount can be changed to liking

Serving
Shot Glass
****

Aladdin Sane recipe

Description
A delicious recipe for Aladdin Sane, with Absolut® Citron vodka, limes, Cointreau® orange liqueur and fruit punch.

Ingredients
1 oz Absolut® Citron vodka
juice of 1/2 limes
1/2 oz Cointreau® orange liqueur
1/4 cup fruit punch

Instructions
Add all ingredients to a cocktail shaker 3/4 filled with ice. Shake, allow to chill for 5 minutes, re-shake, and pour into a martini glass.

Serving
Cocktail Glass
****

Alcoholic Sherbert Delight recipe

Description
A delicious recipe for Alcoholic Sherbert Delight, with Absolut® Mandrin vodka, spiced rum, gin, orange juice and grenadine syrup.

Ingredients
2 oz Absolut® Mandrin vodka
2 oz spiced rum
1 oz gin
5 oz orange juice
2 dashes grenadine syrup

Instructions
Combine the ingredients, starting with the orange juice, in a highball glass. Serve.

Serving
Highball Glass
****

Alebrije recipe

Description
A delicious recipe for Alebrije, with ice, grenadine syrup, Absolut® vodka, Bacardi® white rum, amaretto almond liqueur, gin, white tequila, orange juice and pineapple juice.

Ingredients
ice
1 splash grenadine syrup
1/2 oz Absolut® vodka
1/2 oz Bacardi® white rum

1/2 oz amaretto almond liqueur
1/2 oz gin
1/2 oz white tequila
2 oz orange juice
2 oz pineapple juice

Instructions
First mix some orange juice and pinapple juice in equal parts, and color it with some grenadine (as sweet as you want). This is "conga mix". Fill the glass with ice, add the five licours and mix them, fill the glass with some conga mix and enjoy.

Serving
Hurricane Glass
****

Alien Secretion #2 recipe

Description
A delicious recipe for Alien Secretion #2, with Absolut® vodka, Midori® melon liqueur, Malibu® coconut rum and pineapple juice.

Ingredients
1/4 oz Absolut® vodka
1/4 oz Midori® melon liqueur
1/4 oz Malibu® coconut rum
1/4 oz pineapple juice

Instructions
Add ingredients together in small shaker w/ice. Stir.

Strain into a shot glass.

Serving
Shot Glass
****

Almost Heaven recipe

Description
A delicious recipe for Almost Heaven, with Absolut® Kurant vodka,

amaretto almond liqueur, Chambord® raspberry liqueur, pineapple juice and cranberry juice.

Ingredients
1 - 1/4 oz Absolut® Kurant vodka
3/4 oz amaretto almond liqueur
3/4 oz Chambord® raspberry liqueur
1 splash pineapple juice
1 splash cranberry juice

Instructions
Build in a collins glass over ice.

Serving
Collins Glass
****

Alzheimers recipe

Description
A delicious recipe for Alzheimers, with Canadian Club® whisky, Absolut® Citron vodka and Coca-Cola®.

Ingredients
2 oz Canadian Club® whisky
2 oz Absolut® Citron vodka
1/2 oz Coca-Cola®

Instructions
Combine over ice in a collins glass.

Serving
Collins Glass
****

Apeachy Procaccini recipe

Description
A delicious recipe for Apeachy Procaccini, with Absolut® Apeach vodka

and Juicy Juice® peach juice.

Ingredients
3 oz Absolut® Apeach vodka
3 oz Juicy Juice® peach juice

Instructions
Stir ingredients together in a highball glass filled with ice cubes, and serve.

Serving
Highball Glass
****

Apple Fucker recipe

Description
A delicious recipe for Apple Fucker, with DeKuyper® Sour Apple Pucker schnapps and Absolut® vodka.

Ingredients
1/2 oz DeKuyper® Sour Apple Pucker schnapps
1/2 oz Absolut® vodka

Instructions
Pour the Absolut vodka and DeKuyper Apple Pucker into a shot glass in equal parts, and serve.

Serving
Shot Glass
****

Apple Martini recipe

Description
A delicious recipe for Apple Martini, with Absolut® vodka, DeKuyper® Sour Apple Pucker schnapps and apple juice.

Ingredients

1 part Absolut® vodka
1 part DeKuyper® Sour Apple Pucker schnapps
1 part apple juice

Instructions
Poor all ingredients into a shaker. Shake well and strain into a Martini glass.

Serving
Cocktail Glass
****

Arizona Stingers recipe

Description
A delicious recipe for Arizona Stingers, with Absolut® vodka and iced tea.

Ingredients
2 shots Absolut® vodka
12 oz lemon with iced tea

Instructions
Place ice cubes in the hurricane glass. Add 2 heaping shots of absolut vodka (Note: You can add as many shots of absolut as you want!) Fill the rest of glass with Arizona Iced Tea w/lemon.

Stir to mix using a spoon.

Drink up and enjoy.

Serving
Hurricane Glass
****

Arizona Twister recipe

Description
A delicious recipe for Arizona Twister, with Absolut® vodka, crushed

ice, Malibu® coconut rum, gold tequila, orange juice, pineapple juice, cream of coconut, grenadine syrup and pineapple.

Ingredients
1 shot Absolut® vodka
crushed ice
1 shot Malibu® coconut rum
1 shot gold tequila
1 splash orange juice
1 splash pineapple juice
1 splash cream of coconut
1 squirt grenadine syrup
1 pineapple wedge

Instructions
Mix in the shots of rum, vodka, and tequila.

Add splashes of the three juices, heavy on the pineapple. Top off with grenadine. Crushed ice should already be in glass.

Top off the glass with a pineapple wedge.

Serving
Hurricane Glass
****

Astral Gateway recipe

Description
A delicious recipe for Astral Gateway, with Absolut® vodka, Blue Curacao liqueur, lemon juice, ginger ale and ice.

Ingredients
4 cl Absolut® vodka
2 cl Blue Curacao liqueur
1 cl lemon juice
10 cl ginger ale
fill with ice

Instructions
Put ingredients into the glass, fill with ice.

Serving
Highball Glass
****

AT&T recipe

Description
A delicious recipe for AT&T, with Absolut® vodka, Tanqueray® gin and tonic water.

Ingredients
1 oz Absolut® vodka
1 oz Tanqueray® gin
4 oz tonic water

Instructions
Pour vodka and gin over ice, add tonic water and stir.

Serving
Old-Fashioned Glass
****

Awesome Chandler recipe

Description
A delicious recipe for Awesome Chandler, with Absolut® Mandrin vodka, peach schnapps, amaretto almond liqueur, Midori® melon liqueur, sweet and sour mix, orange juice and cranberry juice.

Ingredients
1 oz Absolut® Mandrin vodka
1 oz peach schnapps
1/4 oz amaretto almond liqueur
1/4 oz Midori® melon liqueur
1 splash sweet and sour mix
orange juice

cranberry juice

Instructions
Pour Absolut Mandrin, peach schnapps, amaretto, Midori melon liqueur and sour mix into a cocktail shaker half-filled with ice cubes. Shake well, and strain into a highball glass filled with ice cubes. Add orange juice and cranberry juice, both to taste. Stir, and serve.

Serving
Highball Glass
****

B.F.D. recipe

Description
A delicious recipe for B.F.D., with Absolut® vodka, triple sec, Everclear® alcohol and grapefruit juice.

Ingredients
1 1/2 oz Absolut® vodka
1 1/2 oz triple sec
1 splash Everclear® alcohol
fill with grapefruit juice

Instructions
Fill glass half full with ice. Add vodka, triple sec, & Everclear. Top off with grapefruit juice.

Serving
Collins Glass
****

Back Shot recipe

Description
A delicious recipe for Back Shot, with Absolut® vodka, sweet and sour mix and Chambord® raspberry liqueur.

Ingredients
2 1/2 oz Absolut® vodka
4 oz sweet and sour mix

1 oz Chambord® raspberry liqueur

Instructions
Stir ingredients over ice.

Serving
Shot Glass
****

Backseat Boogie #2 recipe

Description
A delicious recipe for Backseat Boogie #2, with Absolut® vodka, gin, ginger ale and Ocean Spray® cranberry juice.

Ingredients
1 oz Absolut® vodka
1 oz gin
1 part ginger ale
1 part Ocean Spray® cranberry juice

Instructions
Pour vodka and gin over ice in a collins glass. Fill with equal parts of ginger ale and cranberry juice. Garnish with fruit, and serve.

Serving
Collins Glass
****

Bald Pussy recipe

Description
A delicious recipe for Bald Pussy, with melon liqueur, lime vodka, Absolut® vodka, triple sec, blueberry schnapps, lime juice and 7-Up® soda.

Ingredients
1 1/2 shots melon liqueur
1 shot lime vodka
1 shot Absolut® vodka
1 shot triple sec

1 1/2 shots blueberry schnapps
1 splash lime juice
1 splash 7-Up® soda

Instructions
Pour ingredients over ice in a highball glass and shake.

Serving
Highball Glass
****

Ball of Fun recipe

Description
A delicious recipe for Ball of Fun, with Bacardi® Limon rum, triple sec, Absolut® Citron vodka, fruit punch and ice cubes.

Ingredients
1 liter Bacardi® Limon rum
1 liter triple sec
1 liter Absolut® Citron vodka
2 liters fruit punch
5 lb ice cubes

Instructions
Pour all ingredients into a punch bowl and stir."Drink the fuck up, get fucked up, and break the ball of fun." (BSU)

Serving
Punch Bowl
****

Baltic Murder Mystery recipe

Description
A delicious recipe for Baltic Murder Mystery, with creme de cassis, Absolut® vodka and 7-Up® soda.

Ingredients
1 oz creme de cassis
1 oz Absolut® vodka

fill with 7-Up® soda

Instructions
Pour vodka and creme de cassis in cocktail glass and fill with 7-up. If it is too sweet, try soda water. A slice of lemon compliments the drink quite nicely.

Serving
Cocktail Glass
****

Barbie Shot recipe

Description
A delicious recipe for Barbie Shot, with Malibu® coconut rum, Absolut® vodka, cranberry juice and orange juice.

Ingredients
1 oz Malibu® coconut rum
1 oz Absolut® vodka
1 oz cranberry juice
1 oz orange juice

Instructions
In shaker tin with ice, mix and shake all ingredients.

Serving
Shot Glass
****

Berry Fusion Martini recipe

Description
A delicious recipe for Berry Fusion Martini, with Absolut® Kurant vodka, Hpnotiq® liqueur, creme de cassis and cranberry juice.

Ingredients

1 oz Absolut® Kurant vodka
1/2 oz Hpnotiq® liqueur
1/2 oz creme de cassis
2 oz cranberry juice

Instructions
Add all ingredients to a cocktail shaker half-filled with ice cubes. Shake well and strain into a chilled martini or cocktail glass. Garnish with frozen blueberries placed inside the glass.

Serving
Cocktail Glass
****

Big Dumb Russian recipe

Description
A delicious recipe for Big Dumb Russian, with ice cubes, Absolut® vodka, Sprite® soda, pineapple juice and Maui® Blue Hawaiian schnapps.

Ingredients
ice cubes
2 oz Absolut® vodka
3 parts Sprite® soda
1 splash pineapple juice
Maui® Blue Hawaiian schnapps

Instructions
Fill the glass with ice. I like to use a standard beer glass. Add about 2 shots of vodka. Then fill the glass about 3/4th of the way with Sprite. Then add just a splash of pineapple juice. Finally, add the Blue Maui until you get a faint (almost skyblue) blue color. Stir.

Serving
Beer Mug
****

Bionic Beaver recipe

Description
A delicious recipe for Bionic Beaver, with Absolut® vodka, Busch® lager, Southern Comfort® peach liqueur, 7-Up® soda, sloe gin, orange juice, gin and grenadine syrup.

Ingredients
2 oz Absolut® vodka
12 oz Busch® lager
2 oz Southern Comfort® peach liqueur
7-Up® soda
2 oz sloe gin
orange juice
2 oz gin
2 oz grenadine syrup

Instructions
Put a little crushed ice in the bottom of the pitcher, then the beer, and then the shots. Then top off the pitcher with equal amounts of Orange Juice and 7-Up. Stir.

Serving
Pitcher

****

Bird Bomb recipe

Description
A delicious recipe for Bird Bomb, with Absolut® vodka, DeKuyper® Cheri-Beri Pucker schnapps and lemonade.

Ingredients
3 oz Absolut® vodka
1 oz DeKuyper® Cheri-Beri Pucker schnapps
8 oz lemonade

Instructions
Fill a hurricane glass half-way with ice. Add the Absolut vodka and DeKuyper Cheri-Beri Pucker. Fill with lemonade, and serve.

Serving

Hurricane Glass
****

Bizonkadonk Martini recipe

Description
A delicious recipe for Bizonkadonk Martini, with Absolut® Mandrin vodka, Tanqueray® gin, Tuaca® citrus liqueur, Grand Marnier® orange liqueur, orange juice and Red Bull® energy drink. Also lists similar drink recipe

Ingredients
1 oz Absolut® Mandrin vodka
1/4 oz Tanqueray® gin
1/2 oz Tuaca® citrus liqueur
1/2 oz Grand Marnier® orange liqueur
1 oz fresh orange juice
1/4 - 1/2 oz Red Bull® energy drink

Instructions
Combine the Absolut Mandrin vodka, Tanqueray gin, Tuaca citrus liqueur, Grand Marnier orange liqueur and orange juice in a cocktail shaker half-filled with ice cubes. Strain into a cocktail glass, float Red Bull energy drink on top. Garnish with flamed orange peel, and serve.

Serving
Cocktail Glass
****

Black Martini #2 recipe

Description
A delicious recipe for Black Martini #2, with Absolut® vodka, Chambord® raspberry liqueur, Blue Curacao liqueur and ice.

Ingredients
4 1/2 oz Absolut® vodka
2 oz Chambord® raspberry liqueur
1 oz Blue Curacao liqueur
ice

Instructions
Combine in shaker. Shake vigorously. Strain into cocktail glass.

Serving
Cocktail Glass
****

Black Orgasm recipe

Description
A delicious recipe for Black Orgasm, with sloe gin, Blue Curacao liqueur, peach schnapps and Absolut® vodka.

Ingredients
1/4 shot sloe gin
1/4 shot Blue Curacao liqueur
1/4 shot peach schnapps
1/4 shot Absolut® vodka

Instructions
Just pour, stir, and enjoy.

Serving
Shot Glass
****

Black Swedish Virgin recipe

Description
A delicious recipe for Black Swedish Virgin, with Black Haus® blackberry schnapps, Absolut® vodka, cranberry juice and 7-Up® soda.

Ingredients
1/4 part Black Haus® blackberry schnapps
1/2 part Absolut® vodka
1/4 part cranberry juice
1 splash 7-Up® soda

Instructions
Mix on the rocks.

Serving
Collins Glass
****

Black Widow recipe

Description
A delicious recipe for Black Widow, with Absolut® Citron vodka and Opal Nera® black sambuca.

Ingredients
1 oz Absolut® Citron vodka
1 oz Opal Nera® black sambuca

Instructions
Pour both ingredients over ice and shake. Strain into a martini glass and serve with a lemon twist.

Serving
Cocktail Glass
****

Blackberry Lane recipe

Description
A delicious recipe for Blackberry Lane, with Black Haus® blackberry schnapps, blackberry brandy and Absolut® Kurant vodka.

Ingredients
1/3 oz Black Haus® blackberry schnapps
1/3 oz blackberry brandy
1/3 oz Absolut® Kurant vodka

Instructions
Stir ingredients together in a cocktail shaker over ice. Strain into a shot glass, and serve.

Serving
Shot Glass
****

Blame It On Rio recipe

Description
A delicious recipe for Blame It On Rio, with Absolut® vodka, Captain Morgan® Original spiced rum, Malibu® coconut rum, amaretto almond liqueur, peach schnapps, banana liqueur, pineapple juice and soda water. Also lists similar drin

Ingredients
1/4 oz Absolut® vodka
1/4 oz Captain Morgan® Original spiced rum
1/4 oz Malibu® coconut rum
1/4 oz amaretto almond liqueur
1/4 oz peach schnapps
1/4 oz banana liqueur
1 1/2 oz pineapple juice
soda water

Instructions
Pour the vodka, rum, amaretto, peach schnapps, banana liqueur and pineapple juice into a cocktail shaker half-filled with ice cubes. Shake well. Strain into a highball glass 3/4 filled with ice cubes. Top with soda water, to taste. Squeeze in the juice from a lime wedge and drop the shell into the glass. Serve.

Serving
Highball Glass
****

Blue Chili recipe

Description
A delicious recipe for Blue Chili, with Blue Curacao liqueur, Sprite® soda, Absolut® vodka, gin, white rum and ice.

Ingredients
2 oz Blue Curacao liqueur
1 dash Sprite® soda
1 oz Absolut® vodka
1/2 oz gin
1/2 oz white rum

ice

Instructions
Shake the first 5 ingredients in a shaker. Shake well. Strain into a cocktail class. Add a dash of sprite. Garnish with cherry and lemon reel.

Serving
Cocktail Glass
****

Blue Cosmopolitan recipe

Description
A delicious recipe for Blue Cosmopolitan, with Absolut® Citron vodka, maraschino cherry, Blue Curacao liqueur, grapefruit juice, sugar syrup and sugar.

Ingredients
2 oz Absolut® Citron vodka
1 maraschino cherry
1 oz Blue Curacao liqueur
1/2 oz grapefruit juice
1/2 oz sugar syrup
sugar

Instructions
Frost the rim of a chilled cocktail glass with sugar. Stir absolut citron, blue curacao, grapefruit juice, and sugar syrup in a mixing glass with ice to prevent cloudiness. Strain into cocktail glass. Garnish with a maraschino cherry.

Serving
Cocktail Glass
****

Blue Dragon recipe

Description
A delicious recipe for Blue Dragon, with Absolut® Mandrin vodka and

Blue Curacao liqueur.

Ingredients
3 parts Absolut® Mandrin vodka
1 part Blue Curacao liqueur

Instructions
Mix vodka and blue curacao with crushed ice, shake or stir, and strain into a martini glass. Garnish with orange slice and cherries.

Serving
Cocktail Glass
****

Blue Dragonfly recipe

Description
A delicious recipe for Blue Dragonfly, with Hpnotiq® liqueur, Absolut® vanilla vodka and Sprite® soda.

Ingredients
1 oz Hpnotiq® liqueur
1 oz Absolut® vanilla vodka
1 splash Sprite® soda

Instructions
Combine the Hpnotiq liqueur and Absolut Vanilla vodka over ice in a chilled cocktail glass. Top with Sprite and serve.

Serving
Cocktail Glass
****

Blue Grapes recipe

Description
A delicious recipe for Blue Grapes, with Absolut® Kurant vodka, Kool-Aid® Blue Raspberry mix and Sprite® soda.

Ingredients
1 oz Absolut® Kurant vodka

6 oz Kool-Aid® Blue Raspberry mix
3 oz Sprite® soda

Instructions
Combine Absolut, Kool-Aid and Sprite in a shaker, and shake well. Pour over ice in a collins glass, and serve.

Serving
Collins Glass
****

Blue Haze recipe

Description
A delicious recipe for Blue Haze, with Maui® Blue Hawaiian schnapps, Absolut® Citron vodka and Faygo® Twist soda.

Ingredients
1 liter Maui® Blue Hawaiian schnapps
1 liter Absolut® Citron vodka
4 liters Faygo® Twist soda

Instructions
Stir all ingredients together in a large punch bowl with a large block of ice.

Serving
Punch Bowl
****

Blue MotherFucker recipe

Description
A delicious recipe for Blue MotherFucker, with Absolut® Citron vodka, Blue Curacao liqueur and sweet and sour mix.

Ingredients
3 oz Absolut® Citron vodka
3 oz Blue Curacao liqueur
3 oz sweet and sour mix

Instructions
Shake ingredients, strain over ice in a highball glass, and serve.

Serving
Highball Glass
****

Blue Screw recipe

Description
A delicious recipe for Blue Screw, with Absolut® Mandrin vodka, Blue Curacao liqueur and orange juice.

Ingredients
1 1/2 oz Absolut® Mandrin vodka
1 oz Blue Curacao liqueur
fill with orange juice

Instructions
Fill glass with ice, pour Mandrin and Blue in, then fill it with OJ. Simple.

Serving
Highball Glass
****

Blue Slammer recipe

Description
A delicious recipe for Blue Slammer, with Blue Curacao liqueur, sambuca, Absolut® vodka and lemon juice.

Ingredients
1/2 oz Blue Curacao liqueur
1/2 oz sambuca
1/2 oz Absolut® vodka
1 drop lemon juice

Instructions
Put drop of lemon in first, then add Blue Curacao, and Sambuca. Then slowly add vodka. Sit down, shoot back, and enjoy!

Serving
Shot Glass
****

Blue Solute recipe

Description
A delicious recipe for Blue Solute, with Absolut® vodka, blueberry schnapps and Gatorade® energy drink.

Ingredients
1 1/2 oz Absolut® vodka
1 1/2 oz blueberry schnapps
9 oz blue Gatorade® energy drink

Instructions
Mix ingredients in a highball glass, stir, and serve.

Serving
Highball Glass
****

Bold Gold Monkey recipe

Description
A delicious recipe for Bold Gold Monkey, with gold rum, Absolut® vodka, orange juice and grenadine syrup.

Ingredients
1 part gold rum
1 part Absolut® vodka
4 parts orange juice
1 tsp grenadine syrup

Instructions
Combine all in a shaker with adequate ice. Shake vigorously. Strain into a chilled martini glass.

Serving
Cocktail Glass
****

Boom Shaka Laka recipe

Description
A delicious recipe for Boom Shaka Laka, with triple sec, Absolut® Citron vodka, cranberry juice, Mountain Dew® citrus soda, lemonade and sweet and sour mix.

Ingredients
1 oz triple sec
1 1/2 oz Absolut® Citron vodka
1 splash cranberry juice
1 splash Mountain Dew® citrus soda
1 splash lemonade
2 oz sweet and sour mix

Instructions
Combine ingredients with ice in a margarita glass, mix, and serve.

Serving
Margarita Glass
****

Brain Damage recipe

Description
A delicious recipe for Brain Damage, with Jagermeister® herbal liqueur, Absolut® vodka and dry gin.

Ingredients
2 parts Jagermeister® herbal liqueur
1 part Absolut® vodka
1 1/2 parts dry gin

Instructions
Pour all the ingredients over an ice-cube and stir gently.

Serving
Old-Fashioned Glass
****

Bronx Martini recipe

Description
A delicious recipe for Bronx Martini, with Absolut® Mandrin vodka, sweet vermouth, dry vermouth, sweet and sour mix and orange juice.

Ingredients
1 1/2 oz Absolut® Mandrin vodka
1 splash sweet vermouth
1 splash dry vermouth
1/2 oz sweet and sour mix
4 oz orange juice

Instructions
Mix contents in a martini shaker with ice and serve in a chilled martini glass.

Serving
Cocktail Glass
****

Burberry Bulldog recipe

Description
A delicious recipe for Burberry Bulldog, with Absolut® Kurant vodka, Chambord® raspberry liqueur, Kahlua® coffee liqueur, Irish cream, milk and Dr. Pepper® soda.

Ingredients
1 1/2 oz Absolut® Kurant vodka
1 1/2 oz Chambord® raspberry liqueur
1 1/2 oz Kahlua® coffee liqueur
1 1/2 oz Irish cream
1 - 2 oz milk
1 - 2 oz Dr. Pepper® soda

Instructions
Fill a collins glass with ice cubes. Pour in the vodka, Chambord raspberry liqueur, Kahlua coffee liqueur and Irish cream. Stir, then fill up the glass with equal portions of milk and Dr. Pepper soda. Stir again and serve.

Serving

Collins Glass
****

Buzz Lightyear recipe

Description
A delicious recipe for Buzz Lightyear, with Absolut® vodka, Midori® melon liqueur and orange juice.

Ingredients
2 oz Absolut® vodka
2 oz Midori® melon liqueur
3 oz fresh orange juice

Instructions
Pour over cracked ice filled in glass and stir briefly.

Serving
Collins Glass
****

Cabin Cooler recipe

Description
A delicious recipe for Cabin Cooler, with Absolut® Raspberri vodka, Captain Morgan® Parrot Bay coconut rum, cranberry juice and ginger ale.

Ingredients
16 oz Absolut® Raspberri vodka
16 oz Captain Morgan® Parrot Bay coconut rum
8 oz cranberry juice
4 oz ginger ale

Instructions
Combine all ingredients in a pitcher and chill, preferably in ice. Pour into suitable glasses. Garnish rim of each glass with a lime slice, and serve.

Serving
Pitcher
****

Cactus Cooler recipe

Description
A delicious recipe for Cactus Cooler, with triple sec, Absolut® Mandrin vodka and Rockstar® energy drink.

Ingredients
3/4 oz triple sec
3/4 oz Absolut® Mandrin vodka
8 oz Rockstar® energy drink

Instructions
Fill a shot glass half with triple sec, half mandarin vodka; then drop into a pint glass half-filled with Rockstar energy drink, and serve.

Serving
Beer Mug
****

California Gold Rush recipe

Description
A delicious recipe for California Gold Rush, with 7-Up® soda, Absolut® vodka and Goldschlager® cinnamon schnapps.

Ingredients
12 oz 7-Up® soda
2 oz Absolut® vodka
1 1/2 oz Goldschlager® cinnamon schnapps

Instructions
Pour 7-up into a clear glass without ice. Add vodka and goldschlager, and stir to mix gold flakes evenly through the drink.

Effect: The bubbles of carbon dioxide in the 7-up continuously move the gold flakes around.

Serving
Collins Glass
****

California Lemonade recipe

Description
A delicious recipe for California Lemonade, with 7-Up® soda, Absolut® vodka, Goldschlager® cinnamon schnapps, blended whiskey, lemons, limes, powdered sugar, grenadine syrup and carbonated water.

Ingredients
12 oz 7-Up® soda
2 oz Absolut® vodka
1 1/2 oz Goldschlager® cinnamon schnapps
2 oz blended whiskey
juice of 1 lemons
juice of 1 limes
1 tbsp powdered sugar
1/4 tsp grenadine syrup
carbonated water

Instructions
Shake all ingredients (except carbonated water) with ice and strain into a collins glass over shaved ice. Fill with carbonated water and stir. Decorate with slices of orange and lemon. Add the cherry and serve with a straw.

Serving
Collins Glass
****

Canteloupe Dizzy recipe

Description
A delicious recipe for Canteloupe Dizzy, with Absolut® vodka, Midori® melon liqueur, peach schnapps and club soda.

Ingredients
1 oz Absolut® vodka
1 oz Midori® melon liqueur
1 oz peach schnapps
1 pint club soda

Instructions

Pour club soda into a parfait glass with ice cubes. Pour vodka, melon liquer, and peach schnapps into a shaker and shake well. Strain into the club soda and stir. Garnish with cherry/orange/pineapple.

Serving
Parfait Glass
****

Caribbean Ice Tea recipe

Description
A delicious recipe for Caribbean Ice Tea, with Blue Curacao liqueur, gin, Bacardi® white rum, Jose Cuervo® Especial gold tequila, Absolut® vodka and sweet and sour mix.

Ingredients
1 part Blue Curacao liqueur
1 part gin
1 part Bacardi® white rum
1 part Jose Cuervo® Especial gold tequila
1 part Absolut® vodka
1 part sweet and sour mix

Instructions
Mix all of the ingredients together and serve over ice. Garnish with an orange.

Serving
Hurricane Glass
****

Caucasian recipe

Description
A delicious recipe for Caucasian, with Absolut® vodka, Kahlua® coffee liqueur, half-and-half and ice cubes.

Ingredients
2 oz Absolut® vodka
1 1/2 oz Kahlua® coffee liqueur
1 - 3 oz half-and-half
ice cubes

Instructions
Pour vodka and coffee liqueur (kahlua) over ice cubes. Add desired amount of Half-and-Half.

Serving
Old-Fashioned Glass
****

Chambord Royale recipe

Description
A delicious recipe for Chambord Royale, with Absolut® vodka, Chambord® raspberry liqueur, triple sec and lime juice.

Ingredients
3/4 oz Absolut® vodka
3/4 oz Chambord® raspberry liqueur
1/2 oz triple sec
2 oz lime juice

Instructions
Shake ingredients with ice. Strain into a martini glass, and serve.

Serving
Cocktail Glass
****

Charlie Coke recipe

Description
A delicious recipe for Charlie Coke, with Absolut® vodka and Coca-Cola®.

Ingredients
1 1/2 oz Absolut® vodka

1 bottle Coca-Cola®

Instructions
Add the Absolut Vodka to a cocktail glass filled with ice, top off with Coca-Cola.

Serving
Cocktail Glass
****

Cherry Bomb #2 recipe

Description
A delicious recipe for Cherry Bomb #2, with Absolut® vodka and cherry juice.

Ingredients
1 1/2 oz Absolut® vodka
fill with cherry juice

Instructions
Fill glass with ice. Add the vodka. Fill with unsweetened cherry juice.

Serving
Highball Glass
****

Cherry Lemon Drop recipe

Description
A delicious recipe for Cherry Lemon Drop, with Absolut® Citron vodka, sweet and sour mix, lemon and grenadine syrup.

Ingredients
1 1/2 oz Absolut® Citron vodka
1 1/2 oz sweet and sour mix
1 slice lemon
1 splash grenadine syrup

Instructions
Combine equal parts of Absolut Citron vodka and sweet and sour mix

over ice in a cocktail shaker. Shake well; add juice of one lemon slice and grenadine, then strain into a large shot glass or small old-fashioned glass. Sprinkle sugar around the rim of the shot glass, and serve.

Serving
Shot Glass
****

Cherry Lover recipe

Description
A delicious recipe for Cherry Lover, with cherry brandy, cherry liqueur, maraschino liqueur, Absolut® vodka, ice and club soda.

Ingredients
1 oz cherry brandy
1 oz cherry liqueur
1/2 oz maraschino liqueur
1/2 oz Absolut® vodka
ice
top with club soda

Instructions
Combine the first 5 ingredients into a cocktail shaker. Shake well for 20 seconds. Strain into a cocktail glass. Top with Club Soda.

Serving
Cocktail Glass
****

Chocolate Cake Shooter recipe

Description
A delicious recipe for Chocolate Cake Shooter, with Absolut® Citron vodka, Frangelico® hazelnut liqueur and lemon.

Ingredients
1/2 shot Absolut® Citron vodka
1/2 shot Frangelico® hazelnut liqueur
1 lemon wedge

Instructions
Mix equal parts Absolut Citron and Frangelico into a shot glass. Drink the shot, and follow it immediately by sucking on a sugar-coated lemon wedge.

Serving
Shot Glass
****

Chocolate Martini Lite recipe

Description
A delicious recipe for Chocolate Martini Lite, with Absolut® vodka, creme de cacao, milk and Andes® chocolate mint.

Ingredients
1 oz Absolut® vodka
1 oz creme de cacao
1 1/2 oz milk
1 halved Andes® chocolate mint

Instructions
While chilling a cocktail glass, shake vodka, creme de cacao, and milk. Pour into the chilled cocktail glass over 1/2 chunk of Andes mint chocolate candy, and serve.

Serving
Cocktail Glass
****

Chocolate Orange recipe

Description
A delicious recipe for Chocolate Orange, with Absolut® Mandrin vodka and white creme de cacao.

Ingredients
1 1/2 oz Absolut® Mandrin vodka
1 1/2 oz white creme de cacao

Instructions

Stir with ice, and strain into a chilled cocktail glass. Garnish with shaved chocolate.

Serving
Cocktail Glass
****

Citron My Face recipe

Description
A delicious recipe for Citron My Face, with Absolut® Citron vodka, Grand Marnier® orange liqueur, sweet and sour mix and 7-Up® soda.

Ingredients
1 oz Absolut® Citron vodka
1/2 oz Grand Marnier® orange liqueur
1 - 1/2 oz sweet and sour mix
1 oz 7-Up® soda

Instructions
Mix over ice and strain.

Serving
Shot Glass
****

Citron Splash Martini recipe

Description
A delicious recipe for Citron Splash Martini, with Absolut® Citron vodka, triple sec, lemon juice and sugar.

Ingredients
1 1/2 oz Absolut® Citron vodka
1 1/4 oz triple sec
3/4 oz lemon juice
sugar

Instructions
Combine the Absolut Citron, Triple sec and juice of 1/3 lemon (~3/4 oz juice) in a cocktail shaker half-filled with ice cubes. Shake. Use the

lemon to wet the edge of a chilled martini or cocktail glass, and dip the glass in sugar to coat the rim. Strain the mixture into the cocktail glass, garnish with a lemon twist, and serve.

Serving
Cocktail Glass
****

Citronade recipe

Description
A delicious recipe for Citronade, with lemonade and Absolut® Citron vodka.

Ingredients
8 oz lemonade
3 shots Absolut® Citron vodka

Instructions
Mix lemonade and absolut citron into a collins glass, shake or stir, add ice, and drink.

Serving
Collins Glass
****

Coast-Line recipe

Description
A delicious recipe for Coast-Line, with Blue Curacao liqueur, Absolut® vodka, pineapple juice, 7-Up® soda and cherry.

Ingredients
1/2 oz Blue Curacao liqueur
1/2 oz Absolut® vodka
top with pineapple juice
1 splash 7-Up® soda
1 cherry

Instructions
Pour the blue Curacao and the vodka in a highball glass. Top with pineapple juice and a splash of 7-up. Garnish with a cherry.

Serving
Highball Glass
****

Cold Blood recipe

Description
A delicious recipe for Cold Blood, with Kool-Aid® Blue Raspberry mix, Absolut® Limon vodka, maraschino cherry juice, maraschino cherries and Zima.

Ingredients
Kool-Aid® Blue Raspberry mix
3 oz Absolut® Limon vodka
maraschino cherry juice
maraschino cherries
6 oz Zima

Instructions
Drain the maraschino cherries and set aside the cherry juice. Place the drained cherries in a small bowl and add 3 ounces of Absolut Lemon-flavored vodka. Cover bowl and refridgerate for 72 hours.

When marinated, drain the vodka from the cherries and set aside as a reserve. Reserve the cherries also.

To make one drink:
Fill a hurricane glass one third full of crushed ice. Pour two teaspoons of reserved vodka over the crushed ice. Add 6 ounces of Zima. Fill the glass until 1 inch from the top with blue raspberry Kool-Aid. Add 4 reserved marinated cherries.

Serving
Hurricane Glass
****

Cooter Cork recipe

Description
A delicious recipe for Cooter Cork, with grenadine syrup, Chambord® raspberry liqueur, Aftershock® Hot & Cool cinnamon schnapps and Absolut® Kurant vodka.

Ingredients
1/2 oz grenadine syrup
1/2 oz Chambord® raspberry liqueur
1/4 oz Aftershock® Hot & Cool cinnamon schnapps
1/2 oz Absolut® Kurant vodka

Instructions
Layer ingredients in a tall shot glass in this order: Grenadine, Chambord, Aftershock and Absolut Kurant.

Drink should have varying layers of red.

Serving
Shot Glass
****

Cosmo Katie recipe

Description
A delicious recipe for Cosmo Katie, with Absolut® Kurant vodka, Grand Marnier® orange liqueur, lime juice and cranberry juice.

Ingredients
2 oz Absolut® Kurant vodka
1 oz Grand Marnier® orange liqueur
1 splash lime juice
1 splash cranberry juice

Instructions
Chill cocktail glass. Pour ingredients with ice into mixer and shake well. Serve straight up with a cherry.

Serving
Cocktail Glass
****

Cosmo Kurant recipe

Description
A delicious recipe for Cosmo Kurant, with Absolut® Kurant vodka, Cointreau® orange liqueur, redcurrant juice, raspberry juice and lime juice.

Ingredients
1 1/2 oz Absolut® Kurant vodka
1 oz Cointreau® orange liqueur
1 1/2 oz redcurrant juice
1 1/2 oz raspberry juice
1 oz lime juice

Instructions
Combine all ingredients in a cocktail shaker half-filled with ice cubes. Shake well, and strain into a cocktail or martini glass. Garnish with a lime wedge on the rim, and serve.

Serving
Cocktail Glass
****

Cosmobellini recipe

Description
A delicious recipe for Cosmobellini, with Absolut® Citron vodka, Cointreau® orange liqueur, lime, cranberry juice, peach puree and Prosecco® sparkling wine.

Ingredients
1 oz Absolut® Citron vodka
1/2 oz Cointreau® orange liqueur
1 lime wedge
1 splash cranberry juice
1/2 oz white peach puree
Prosecco® sparkling wine

Instructions
Pour vodka and cointreau into a shaker. Squeeze in the juice of one wedge of lime. Add peach puree, a splash of cranberry juice, and shake.

Strain into a cocktail glass, top with prosecco and serve.

Serving
Cocktail Glass
****

Cosmopolitan Cocktail #2 recipe

Description
A delicious recipe for Cosmopolitan Cocktail #2, with Absolut® Citron vodka, lime juice, triple sec and cranberry juice.

Ingredients
1 1/4 oz Absolut® Citron vodka
1/4 oz lime juice
1/4 oz triple sec
1/4 cup cranberry juice

Instructions
Combine all ingredients in a cocktail shaker with ice. Shake briefly and pour into a chilled cocktail glass. Garnish with a lime twist.

Serving
Cocktail Glass
****

Cosmopolitan Cocktail #4 recipe

Description
A delicious recipe for Cosmopolitan Cocktail #4, with Absolut® Citron vodka, Cointreau® orange liqueur and cranberry juice.

Ingredients
1 1/2 oz Absolut® Citron vodka
3/4 oz Cointreau® orange liqueur
1 oz cranberry juice

Instructions
Combine all ingredients in a cocktail or martini shaker with ice and 2 squeezed lime wedges. Shake violently for 10 seconds. Strain into a martini or cocktail glass garnished with a lemon twist, and serve.

Serving
Cocktail Glass
****

Cossak recipe

Description
A delicious recipe for Cossak, with Absolut® vodka, Kahlua® coffee liqueur, Godiva® chocolate liqueur and milk.

Ingredients
1 shot Absolut® vodka
1 shot Kahlua® coffee liqueur
1 shot Godiva® chocolate liqueur
2 cups milk

Instructions
Add liqueur after filling glass with preferred amount of milk. Vodka can be excluded for a milder drink.

Serving
Coffee Mug
****

Country Time recipe

Description
A delicious recipe for Country Time, with Absolut® Citron vodka, vodka, raspberry schnapps, Sprite® soda and lemon.

Ingredients
1 oz Absolut® Citron vodka
1 oz vodka
1/2 oz raspberry schnapps
1 splash Sprite® soda
2 lemon wedges

Instructions
Mix vodkas, lemon juice, and raspberry schnapps together in a cocktail shaker half-filled with ice cubes. Shake until very cold. Strain into a

large shot glass. Top with a splash of sprite, and serve.

Serving
Shot Glass
****

Cowboy Killer recipe

Description
A delicious recipe for Cowboy Killer, with Captain Morgan® Original spiced rum, Absolut® vodka and Jagermeister® herbal liqueur.

Ingredients
1/3 oz Captain Morgan® Original spiced rum
1/3 oz Absolut® vodka
1/3 oz Jagermeister® herbal liqueur

Instructions
Stir ingredients together in a shot glass, and serve.

Serving
Shot Glass
****

Crantini recipe

Description
A delicious recipe for Crantini, with Absolut® vodka, triple sec, vermouth, cranberry juice, ice cubes and cranberry.

Ingredients
1 1/2 oz Absolut® vodka
1/2 oz triple sec
1/2 oz vermouth
4 oz cranberry juice
ice cubes
cranberry

Instructions

Add all the ingredients in a martini shaker with ice. Then shake, pour into martini glass and add a few cranberries to complete the drink.(Soak the cranberries in vodka first)

Serving
Cocktail Glass
****

Creamsicle #4 recipe

Description
A delicious recipe for Creamsicle #4, with Absolut® Citron vodka, orange juice and grenadine syrup.

Ingredients
1 oz Absolut® Citron vodka
2 oz orange juice
1 tsp grenadine syrup

Instructions
Place about 4 ice cubes in a cocktail glass. Pour in Absolut Citron and fill the glass around three-quarters of the way with orange juice. Top off with grenadine, stir and serve.

Serving
Cocktail Glass
****

Crimson Tide recipe

Description
A delicious recipe for Crimson Tide, with Absolut® vodka, Malibu® coconut rum, Chambord® raspberry liqueur, Maui® Blue Hawaiian schnapps, Southern Comfort® peach liqueur, Bacardi® 151 rum, cranberry juice an

Ingredients
1/4 oz Absolut® vodka
1/4 oz Malibu® coconut rum
1/4 oz Chambord® raspberry liqueur
1/4 oz Maui® Blue Hawaiian schnapps

1/4 oz Southern Comfort® peach liqueur
1/4 oz Bacardi® 151 rum
1/4 oz cranberry juice
1/4 oz Sprite® soda

Instructions
Combine all ingrediants, chill over ice, strain.

****

Crooked Monkey recipe

Description
A delicious recipe for Crooked Monkey, with Absolut® vodka, Irish whiskey, orange juice and 7-Up® soda.

Ingredients
1 shot 100 proof Absolut® vodka
1 shot Irish whiskey
orange juice
7-Up® soda

Instructions
Fill beer mug with ice. Add all ingredients and stir.

Serving
Beer Mug
****

Cruz Azul recipe

Description
A delicious recipe for Cruz Azul, with 151 proof rum, Bacardi® Limon rum, Absolut® Citron vodka, Rumple Minze® peppermint liqueur and Blue Curacao liqueur.

Ingredients
1 oz 151 proof rum
1 oz Bacardi® Limon rum
1 oz Absolut® Citron vodka
1 oz Rumple Minze® peppermint liqueur

1 oz Blue Curacao liqueur

Instructions
Stir and serve.

Serving
Shot Glass
****

Cry Baby Blues recipe

Description
A delicious recipe for Cry Baby Blues, with strawberry guava juice, Blue Curacao liqueur and Absolut® vodka.

Ingredients
4 1/2 oz strawberry guava juice
1 oz Blue Curacao liqueur
1 oz Absolut® vodka

Instructions
Serve with shaved ice.

Serving
Hurricane Glass
****

Cucaracha #2 recipe

Description
A delicious recipe for Cucaracha #2, with Absolut® vodka and Kahlua® coffee liqueur.

Ingredients
3 parts Absolut® vodka
1 part Kahlua® coffee liqueur

Instructions
Use a shot-glass and fill to the above proportions. Light the drink on fire. (It helps if you move the lighter in a circular pattern around the top of the drink.) Shoot it through a straw. Be careful!

Serving
Shot Glass
****

Cum Scorcher recipe

Description
A delicious recipe for Cum Scorcher, with butterscotch schnapps, Absolut® vodka, Kahlua® coffee liqueur and Carolans® Irish cream.

Ingredients
1 tbsp butterscotch schnapps
1 tbsp Absolut® vodka
1 tbsp Kahlua® coffee liqueur
1 dash Carolans® Irish cream

Instructions
In a shot glass put butterscotch schnapps, vodka and kahlua in that order. Slowly add the irish cream.

*A little extra irish cream may be used to allow the drink to stand and the mix to get scorched.

Serving
Shot Glass
****

Currant Fuzzy Navel recipe

Description
A delicious recipe for Currant Fuzzy Navel, with Absolut® Kurant vodka, peach schnapps and orange juice.

Ingredients
1 oz Absolut® Kurant vodka
1 oz peach schnapps
6 oz orange juice

Instructions
Pour all ingredients into a cocktail shaker half-filled with ice cubes.

Shake well, strain into a highball glass, and serve.

Serving
Highball Glass
****

D & D Lay recipe

Description
A delicious recipe for D & D Lay, with Jagermeister® herbal liqueur, Absolut® Citron vodka and lemonade.

Ingredients
1 oz Jagermeister® herbal liqueur
1 oz Absolut® Citron vodka
10 oz lemonade

Instructions
Serve shaken, not stirred.

Serving
Collins Glass
****

Dea Lea recipe

Description
A delicious recipe for Dea Lea, with Absolut® vodka, coconut liqueur, amaretto almond liqueur and vanilla liqueur.

Ingredients
1 oz Absolut® vodka
1 oz coconut liqueur
1 oz amaretto almond liqueur
1 oz vanilla liqueur

Instructions
Shake ingredients with ice and strain over ice cubes in a chilled cocktail glass.

Serving

Cocktail Glass
****

Deep Blue recipe

Description
A delicious recipe for Deep Blue, with Absolut® vodka, Bols® Blue Curacao liqueur and Champagne.

Ingredients
3 cl Absolut® vodka
1 cl Bols® Blue Curacao liqueur
2 cl Champagne

Instructions
Stir vodka and blue curacao together with ice in a glass. Top with champagne, and drop a blue maraschino cherry to the bottom.

Serving
Cocktail Glass
****

Dephaekt recipe

Description
A delicious recipe for Dephaekt, with Absolut® Kurant vodka, orgeat syrup, Frangelico® hazelnut liqueur, cranberry juice and Sprite® soda.

Ingredients
4 cl Absolut® Kurant vodka
1 1/2 cl orgeat syrup
1 cl Frangelico® hazelnut liqueur
fill with 2/3 cranberry juice
fill with 1/3 Sprite® soda

Instructions
Blend the absolut kurant, oregat and frangelico in a mixer. Pour in highball glass, add 2 ice cubes, fill with the cranberry juice and sprite. Put a slice of lemon on the edge of the glass.

Optional - add a dash of lime for an even fresher taste.

Serving
Highball Glass
****

Dib Dab recipe

Description
A delicious recipe for Dib Dab, with Absolut® Citron vodka, Absolut® Mandrin vodka, Sourz® Tropical Blue liqueur, sweet and sour mix, lime and lemonade.

Ingredients
1/2 oz Absolut® Citron vodka
1/2 oz Absolut® Mandrin vodka
1 1/2 oz Sourz® Tropical Blue liqueur
1 oz sweet and sour mix
3 fresh, squeezed lime wedges
lemonade

Instructions
Fill a hurricane glass with ice add all ingredients. Shake or stir vigorously. Top with lemonade, to taste, and serve.

Serving
Hurricane Glass
****

Dick Hard recipe

Description
A delicious recipe for Dick Hard, with Absolut® vodka, Tanqueray® gin, Bacardi® white rum and Sprite® soda.

Ingredients
1 oz Absolut® vodka
1 oz Tanqueray® gin
1 oz Bacardi® white rum
fill with Sprite® soda

Instructions

Mix all three liquors then fill with sprite. Garnish with lime, and serve.

Serving
Highball Glass
****

Dignified Iced Tea recipe

Description
A delicious recipe for Dignified Iced Tea, with ice cubes, Absolut® Citron vodka and iced tea.

Ingredients
3 ice cubes
2 oz Absolut® Citron vodka
4 oz iced tea

Instructions
Use absolut citron or other citrus flavored vodka. Mix in highball glass and enjoy.

Serving
Highball Glass
****

Diva recipe

Description
A delicious recipe for Diva, with Absolut® vodka, passion-fruit juice, lime juice, cherry juice and 7-Up® soda.

Ingredients
1 1/2 oz Absolut® vodka
1/2 oz passion-fruit juice
1/2 oz lime juice
1 tbsp cherry juice
fill with 7-Up® soda

Instructions
Pour and build in a tall glass or collins glass. Fill with 7-up. Garnish with cherry and lime.

Serving
Collins Glass
****

Doggystyle recipe

Description
A delicious recipe for Doggystyle, with coconut rum, Absolut® Raspberri vodka and Sprite® soda.

Ingredients
1 oz coconut rum
1 oz Absolut® Raspberri vodka
6 oz Sprite® soda

Instructions
Pour all ingredients into a collins glass filled with crushed ice. Stir well, and serve.

Serving
Collins Glass
****

Don Roberto recipe

Description
A delicious recipe for Don Roberto, with Absolut® Mandrin vodka, blackberry brandy and 7-Up® soda.

Ingredients
3/4 oz Absolut® Mandrin vodka
1/4 oz blackberry brandy
5 oz 7-Up® soda

Instructions
Pour ingredients into a highball glass half-filled with ice cubes. Stir gently, and serve.

Serving

Highball Glass
****

Donna Reed recipe

Description
A delicious recipe for Donna Reed, with Absolut® vodka, cranberry juice and sweet and sour mix.

Ingredients
2 oz Absolut® vodka
4 oz cranberry juice
4 oz sweet and sour mix

Instructions
Pour cranberry juice (more or less to taste) and sour mix over one cup of crushed ice in a blender. Blend for a few seconds, add vodka and blend again until frothy. Serve in a cocktail or margarita glass, or freeze until slushy.

Serving
Margarita Glass
****

Double Fudge Martini #2 recipe

Description
A delicious recipe for Double Fudge Martini #2, with Absolut® vodka, Kahlua® coffee liqueur, espresso, chocolate topping, DeKuyper® Buttershots liqueur, cream and chocolate.

Ingredients
1 1/2 oz Absolut® vodka
1/2 oz Kahlua® coffee liqueur
1/2 tsp espresso ground coffee
1 1/2 oz chocolate topping
1/3 oz DeKuyper® Buttershots liqueur
1 1/2 - 2 oz cream
1 tsp grated chocolate

Instructions

Shake the Absolut vodka, Kahlua coffee liqueur, espresso coffee and chocolate topping with ice and strain into a chilled cocktail glass. In a fresh shaker, shake cream and DeKuyper Buttershots (butterscotch liqueur) until thickened and float on top of the chocolate mix. Garnish with grated chocolate and chocoloate topping, and serve.

Serving
Cocktail Glass
****

Dry Lemonade recipe

Description
A delicious recipe for Dry Lemonade, with Absolut® Citron vodka, lime juice, sugar and 7-Up® soda.

Ingredients
1 oz Absolut® Citron vodka
1 tbsp lime juice
1 tsp sugar
2 1/2 oz 7-Up® soda

Instructions
Pour the Absolut Citron into an 8-oz highball glass filled with ice cubes. Fill with 7-up, and add lime juice. Sweeten with sugar. Top with a twist of lemon, and serve.

Serving
Highball Glass
****

Eagle Eye recipe

Description
A delicious recipe for Eagle Eye, with Absolut® vodka, Passoa® liqueur, orange juice, cranberry juice and ice.

Ingredients
3 cl Absolut® vodka
3 cl Passoa® liqueur
1/2 part orange juice

1/2 part cranberry juice
ice

Instructions
Shake and serve in a highball glass with ice. Garnish with a slice of lime on the rim of the glass.

Serving
Highball Glass
****

Ejhazz recipe

Description
A delicious recipe for Ejhazz, with Absolut® vodka, Dole® orchard peach juice, vanilla and ice.

Ingredients
1 1/2 oz Absolut® vodka
3 oz Dole® orchard peach juice
1 - 3 drops vanilla
ice

Instructions
Add vodka and peach juice. Fill glass with ice and add vanilla to taste. If the drink is too sweet, dilute it with water.

Serving
Old-Fashioned Glass
****

Electric Lemonade recipe

Description
A delicious recipe for Electric Lemonade, with Absolut® Citron vodka, Orange Curacao liqueur, lemonade and strawberries.

Ingredients
1 1/4 oz Absolut® Citron vodka
1/2 oz Orange Curacao liqueur
4 oz lemonade

1 tbsp pureed strawberries

Instructions
Blend with ice until smooth. Serve in a hurricane glass and garnish with a lemon wheel.

Serving
Hurricane Glass
****

En Sann En recipe

Description
A delicious recipe for En Sann En, with Absolut® vodka, sweet and sour mix and Coca-Cola®.

Ingredients
4 cl Absolut® vodka
4 cl sweet and sour mix
Coca-Cola®

Instructions
Fill long drinks glass with ice-cubes, add vodka and sour-mix. Top with coca-cola, stir.

Serving
Collins Glass
****

Enigma recipe

Description
A delicious recipe for Enigma, with Malibu® coconut rum, Absolut® vodka, triple sec, Southern Comfort® peach liqueur, amaretto almond liqueur, orange juice, cranberry juice and grenadine syrup.

Ingredients
1 oz Malibu® coconut rum
1 oz Absolut® vodka
1 oz triple sec
1 oz Southern Comfort® peach liqueur

1 oz amaretto almond liqueur
1 splash orange juice
1 splash cranberry juice
1 splash grenadine syrup

Instructions
Pour the rum, vodka, triple sec, Southern Comfort and amaretto into a collins glass filled with ice cubes. Add a splash of orange juice and cranberry juice. Top with a splash of grenadine. Stir well, and serve.

Serving
Collins Glass
****

Epidural recipe

Description
A delicious recipe for Epidural, with Everclear® alcohol, Absolut® vodka, Malibu® coconut rum and coconut cream.

Ingredients
1 part Everclear® alcohol
1 part Absolut® vodka
1 part Malibu® coconut rum
1 part coconut cream

Instructions
Chill all ingredients well. Mix equal parts and serve in a cordial glass. Or, if you have a test tube or beaker handy, go for it!

Serving
Cordial Glass
****

Erictini recipe

Description
A delicious recipe for Erictini, with Absolut® vodka, Cointreau® orange liqueur, strawberry juice, lemon juice, cream soda, Archers® peach schnapps and grenadine syrup.

Ingredients
1 oz Absolut® vodka
1 oz Cointreau® orange liqueur
2 oz strawberry juice
1 splash lemon juice
1 oz cream soda
1/2 oz Archers® peach schnapps
1 splash grenadine syrup

Instructions
Pour all ingredients into a cocktail shaker half-filled with cracked ice. Shake well. Strain into a chilled cocktail glass. Pour a splash of grenadine syrup on top and serve.

Serving
Cocktail Glass
****

Esirnus recipe

Description
A delicious recipe for Esirnus, with Absolut® vodka, Chambord® raspberry liqueur, Midori® melon liqueur, Sprite® soda and maraschino cherry.

Ingredients
1 shot Absolut® vodka
2 shots Chambord® raspberry liqueur
2 shots Midori® melon liqueur
Sprite® soda
1 maraschino cherry

Instructions
Pour midori and chambord over ice in a glass and stir. Partially fill the glass with Sprite. Stir in vodka and add the maraschino cherry.

Serving
Old-Fashioned Glass
****

Espresso Martini recipe

Description
A delicious recipe for Espresso Martini, with espresso, Absolut® vodka, Kahlua® coffee liqueur and white creme de cacao.

Ingredients
1 oz cold espresso
1 1/2 oz Absolut® vodka
1 1/2 oz Kahlua® coffee liqueur
1 oz white creme de cacao

Instructions
Pour ingredients into shaker filled with ice, shake vigorously, and strain into chilled martini glass. It should be somewhat frothy.

Serving
Cocktail Glass
****

Estonian Forest-Fire recipe

Description
A delicious recipe for Estonian Forest-Fire, with Absolut® vodka, Tabasco® sauce and kiwi.

Ingredients
1 oz chilled Absolut® vodka
12 drops Tabasco® sauce
1 slice kiwi

Instructions
Add vodka to a shot glass. Drop in the tabasco sauce, and chase with the kiwi.

Serving

Shot Glass
****

Evil Corona recipe

Description
A delicious recipe for Evil Corona, with Absolut® Citron vodka, Corona® Extra lager and lime.

Ingredients
2 oz Absolut® Citron vodka
1 bottle Corona® Extra lager
1 lime wedge

Instructions
Pour (drink) the first 2 oz. of corona, and add 2 oz. of Absolut Citron. Cap top of bottle and turn upside down for about 5 seconds. Serve with a lime wedge.

****

Fahrenheit 5000 recipe

Description
A delicious recipe for Fahrenheit 5000, with Firewater® cinnamon schnapps, Absolut® Peppar vodka and Tabasco® sauce.

Ingredients
1/2 oz Firewater® cinnamon schnapps
1/2 oz Absolut® Peppar vodka
1 dash Tabasco® sauce

Instructions
Cover bottom of shot glass with tabasco sauce and then fill with half firewater and half absolut peppar.

Serving
Shot Glass
****

Federal Law recipe

Description
A delicious recipe for Federal Law, with Absolut® Kurant vodka, Chambord® raspberry liqueur, sweet and sour mix, cranberry juice and tonic water.

Ingredients
1 1/2 oz Absolut® Kurant vodka
1 1/2 oz Chambord® raspberry liqueur
1 1/2 oz sweet and sour mix
4 oz cranberry juice
1 splash tonic water

Instructions
Fill a short glass with ice cubes. Add the Absolut Kurant vodka, Chambord raspberry liqueur, sour mix and cranberry juice. Stir well. Splash tonic water; stir again. Garnish as desired, and serve.

Serving
Cocktail Glass
****

Feel This recipe

Description
A delicious recipe for Feel This, with Absolut® vodka, sloe gin, pineapple juice, Southern Comfort® peach liqueur, Midori® melon liqueur and ice cubes.

Ingredients
1 oz Absolut® vodka
1 1/2 oz sloe gin
fill with pineapple juice
1/2 oz Southern Comfort® peach liqueur
1/2 oz Midori® melon liqueur
ice cubes

Instructions
Fill glass with ice. Next add absolut, sloe gin, pineapple juice, southern comfort, and last midori. Add pineapple and cherry garnish.

Serving

Collins Glass
****

Flaming Jesus recipe

Description
A delicious recipe for Flaming Jesus, with Absolut® vodka, lime juice, grenadine syrup and Bacardi® 151 rum.

Ingredients
1 1/2 oz Absolut® vodka
1 splash lime juice
1 splash grenadine syrup
Bacardi® 151 rum

Instructions
Pour vodka, lime juice, and grenadine into shot glass. Then layer 151 proof rum on top from the back of a spoon. Light the 151 and shoot it while lit if you dare. If you are worried about shooting a lit drink, just blow out the flame and then shoot the drink.

Serving
Shot Glass
****

Flaming Lemon Drop recipe

Description
A delicious recipe for Flaming Lemon Drop, with Absolut® Citron vodka, Galliano® herbal liqueur, lemon, sugar and 151 proof rum.

Ingredients
1 1/2 shots Absolut® Citron vodka
1 splash Galliano® herbal liqueur
1/2 slice lemon
1/4 tsp sugar
1/4 tsp 151 proof rum

Instructions
Pour absolut citron into a shot glass and top off with a splash of galliano. Place one half lemon slice flat on the rim of the shot glass, put some

sugar on the slice and soak the sugar with 151 proof rum.
--
Just before drinking, ignite the sugar. Blow the flame out when it seems to caramelize the sugar. Lick the sugar off the lemon slice, down the vodka mixture, then either suck the juices or bite the pulp of the lemon.

Serving
Shot Glass
****

Flaming Lemon recipe

Description
A delicious recipe for Flaming Lemon, with Absolut® Citron vodka, lemon juice and Everclear® alcohol.

Ingredients
1 oz Absolut® Citron vodka
3/4 oz lemon juice
1 tsp Everclear® alcohol

Instructions
Squeeze half a lemon into a mixing glass, and add the Absolut Citron. Mix them together, and pour into a shot glass. Spoon the Everclear over the surface of the mixture, light on fire, and serve.

Serving
Shot Glass
****

Foreplay on the Neutral Ground recipe

Description
A delicious recipe for Foreplay on the Neutral Ground, with Absolut® vodka, Midori® melon liqueur, pineapple juice, cranberry juice and ice.

Ingredients
8 oz Absolut® vodka
4 oz Midori® melon liqueur
12 oz pineapple juice
12 oz cranberry juice

ice

Instructions
Fill glasses with ice. Mix absolut, midori, pineapple juice and cranberry juice in a decanter. Pour over ice and serve. Makes several.

Serving
Hurricane Glass
****

Forest Funk recipe

Description
A delicious recipe for Forest Funk, with Absolut® Citron vodka, Archers® peach schnapps and grapefruit juice.

Ingredients
1 1/2 oz Absolut® Citron vodka
3/4 oz Archers® peach schnapps
grapefruit juice

Instructions
Moisten the rim of the collins glass with a lime wedge and coat the rim with granulated sugar. Ice the glass and build the vodka and peach schnapps. Top with grapefruit juice.

Serving
Collins Glass
****

Fox Poison recipe

Description
A delicious recipe for Fox Poison, with Absolut® vodka, Blue Curacao liqueur, lime juice, grenadine syrup and Sprite® soda.

Ingredients
4 cl Absolut® vodka
2 cl Blue Curacao liqueur

2 cl lime juice
1 splash grenadine syrup
fill with Sprite® soda

Instructions
Begin with vodka, then blue curacao. After that, add the lime liqueur. Mix in the grenadine. Stir gently. Fill up with sprite and put in some ice cubes.

Serving
Hurricane Glass
****

Fraustadt recipe

Description
A delicious recipe for Fraustadt, with Absolut® vodka, Cointreau® orange liqueur, Midori® melon liqueur and lemon juice.

Ingredients
2 cl Absolut® vodka
2 cl Cointreau® orange liqueur
2 cl Midori® melon liqueur
fill with lemon juice

Instructions
Fill the boston shaker with all the ingredients and a lot of ice cubes, then shake untill your hand goes cold. Pour up in a highball glass and put a lemon slice on the edge.

Serving
Highball Glass
****

French Cosmopolitan recipe

Description
A delicious recipe for French Cosmopolitan, with Absolut® Citron vodka, Grand Marnier® orange liqueur, sweet and sour mix, cranberry juice, lime juice and grenadine syrup.

Ingredients
1 oz Absolut® Citron vodka
1/2 oz Grand Marnier® orange liqueur
1/2 oz sweet and sour mix
1/2 oz cranberry juice
1/4 oz lime juice
1 drop grenadine syrup

Instructions
Pour all ingredients (except grenadine) into a shaker, shake well and strain into a chilled large martini glass. Pour a drop of grenadine into the middle of the glass and let it fall to bottom. (It will color the stem red.) Garnish with a slice of lime, and serve.

Serving
Cocktail Glass
****

French Flamingo recipe

Description
A delicious recipe for French Flamingo, with Absolut® Kurant vodka, Cointreau® orange liqueur, lime juice and pomegranate juice.

Ingredients
1 oz Absolut® Kurant vodka
1 oz Cointreau® orange liqueur
3/4 oz fresh lime juice
3/4 oz fresh pomegranate juice

Instructions
Shake ingredients well with ice and strain into a chilled cocktail glass. Garnish with a twist of lime peel, and serve.

Serving
Cocktail Glass
****

French Sailor recipe

Description
A delicious recipe for French Sailor, with Cointreau® orange liqueur, Absolut® Citron vodka and sugar.

Ingredients
1 part Cointreau® orange liqueur
1 part Absolut® Citron vodka
1 sugar cube

Instructions
Mix warm cointreau and vodka into a tumbler with a cube of sugar. Stir until sugar is dissolved.

Serving
Old-Fashioned Glass
****

Fruity Screaming Fuzzy Navel recipe

Description
A delicious recipe for Fruity Screaming Fuzzy Navel, with orange juice, peach schnapps, Absolut® vodka and strawberry daiquiri mix.

Ingredients
64 oz orange juice
8 oz peach schnapps
8 oz Absolut® vodka
4 bottles strawberry daiquiri mix

Instructions
Pour orange juice and peach schnapps in a punch bowl. Add the vodka. Pour the bottles of strawberry daiquiri mix in after. Stir a little. Serve.

Serving
Punch Bowl
****

Fucking Hot recipe

Description
A delicious recipe for Fucking Hot, with Absolut® Peppar vodka and DeKuyper® Hot Damn cinnamon schnapps.

Ingredients
1 1/2 oz Absolut® Peppar vodka
1 1/2 oz DeKuyper® Hot Damn cinnamon schnapps

Instructions
Pour both ingredients into an old-fashioned glass, stir briefly and serve.

Serving
Old-Fashioned Glass
****

Funky Cold Medina recipe

Description
A delicious recipe for Funky Cold Medina, with Absolut® vodka, Southern Comfort® peach liqueur, Blue Curacao liqueur, cranberry juice and ice.

Ingredients
1 oz Absolut® vodka
1 oz Southern Comfort® peach liqueur
1 oz Blue Curacao liqueur
top with cranberry juice
ice

Instructions
Pour over ice and top off with cranberry juice.

Serving
Mason Jar
****

Funky Filly recipe

Description
A delicious recipe for Funky Filly, with Absolut® vodka, Midori® melon liqueur, wild cherry liqueur, triple sec, cranberry juice, lemon-

lime soda and lime juice.

Ingredients
3/4 oz Absolut® vodka
3/4 oz Midori® melon liqueur
3/4 oz wild cherry liqueur
3/4 oz triple sec
2 oz cranberry juice
2 oz lemon-lime soda
1 jigger lime juice

Instructions
Mix ingredients and strain over ice.

Serving
Hurricane Glass
****

Funnel Cloud recipe

Description
A delicious recipe for Funnel Cloud, with beer, ginger ale, Absolut® vodka, light rum and amaretto almond liqueur.

Ingredients
40 oz beer
12 oz ginger ale
1/4 shot Absolut® vodka
1/4 shot light rum
1/2 shot amaretto almond liqueur

Instructions
Pour beer, ginger ale, vodka, light rum, and amaretto in a funnel. Turn the funnel while you drink it.

****

Fuquay Friday Night recipe

Description
A delicious recipe for Fuquay Friday Night, with Absolut® Kurant

vodka, Sprite® soda, grenadine syrup and cherry cola.

Ingredients
2 shots Absolut® Kurant vodka
2 shots Sprite® soda
2 tbsp grenadine syrup
1 shot cherry cola

Instructions
Add absolut kurant and sprite to a cocktail glass. Mix in the grenadine syrup, and add the cherry cola. Serve. Add a dash of lime for a slightly different taste.

Serving
Cocktail Glass
****

Fuzzy Ass recipe

Description
A delicious recipe for Fuzzy Ass, with Absolut® Citron vodka, DeKuyper® Peachtree schnapps, sweet and sour mix, grenadine syrup, triple sec and Sprite® soda.

Ingredients
2 oz Absolut® Citron vodka
1 1/2 oz DeKuyper® Peachtree schnapps
1 oz sweet and sour mix
1 tsp grenadine syrup
1 oz triple sec
fill with Sprite® soda

Instructions
Combine all ingredients into a large strainer/mixer. Add a handful of ice. Shake for a few seconds. Strain into a mason jar.

Serving
Mason Jar
****

Fuzzy Balls recipe

Description
A delicious recipe for Fuzzy Balls, with Absolut® Citron vodka, Bacardi® Limon rum, peach schnapps and 7-Up® soda.

Ingredients
1 part Absolut® Citron vodka
1 part Bacardi® Limon rum
1 part peach schnapps
fill with 7-Up® soda

Instructions
Mix alcoholic ingredients one part each - and add 7-up. Eight shots of each requires a 2L bottle of 7-up.

Serving
Punch Bowl
****

Fuzzy Martini recipe

Description
A delicious recipe for Fuzzy Martini, with Absolut® vodka, peach schnapps and peach.

Ingredients
2 1/2 oz Absolut® vodka
1 oz peach schnapps
1 slice peach

Instructions
Combine vodka and schnapps over lots of ice. Stir and pour into chilled martini glass. Garnish with fresh slice of peach.

Serving
Cocktail Glass
****

Fuzzy Nuts recipe

Description
A delicious recipe for Fuzzy Nuts, with Absolut® Citron vodka, gin and

Sunny Delight® orange juice.

Ingredients
1 1/2 oz Absolut® Citron vodka
1 1/2 oz gin
3 oz chilled Sunny Delight® orange juice

Instructions
Pour all ingredients into a highball glass filled with ice cubes. Stir well, and serve.

Serving
Highball Glass
****

G Bomb recipe

Description
A delicious recipe for G Bomb, with Goldschlager® cinnamon schnapps and Absolut® vodka.

Ingredients
1/2 shot Goldschlager® cinnamon schnapps
1/2 shot Absolut® vodka

Instructions
Chill both ingredients by placing the bottles in the freezer for at least 1 hour. You should also chill the shot glasses you will be using the same way. Pour both ingredients into a chilled shot glass and enjoy.

Serving
Shot Glass
****

Gailwarning recipe

Description
A delicious recipe for Gailwarning, with Absolut® vodka, Sprite® soda and lemon juice.

Ingredients

6 cl Absolut® vodka
6 cl Sprite® soda
1 cl lemon juice

Instructions
Pour vodka over ice in a collins glass. Add sprite and top with lemon juice. Garnish with a lemon slice.

Serving
Collins Glass
****

Get Faced recipe

Description
A delicious recipe for Get Faced, with Bacardi® 151 rum, Absolut® Citron vodka, gin and Coca-Cola®.

Ingredients
1 part Bacardi® 151 rum
1 part Absolut® Citron vodka
1 part gin
1 part Coca-Cola®

Instructions
Pour contents on ice pour into shaker give one hard shake then pour back into glass serve chilled
****

Getaway Car recipe

Description
A delicious recipe for Getaway Car, with peach schnapps and Absolut® Citron vodka.

Ingredients
3/4 oz peach schnapps
1/4 oz Absolut® Citron vodka

Instructions
Mix in a shot glass.

Serving
Shot Glass
****

Geting recipe

Description
A delicious recipe for Geting, with Absolut® vodka, banana liqueur and ginger ale.

Ingredients
2 cl Absolut® vodka
1 cl banana liqueur
fill with ginger ale

Instructions
Start with the ice, add the vodka then the liquor then the ginger ale.

Serving
Highball Glass
****

Gingervitas recipe

Description
A delicious recipe for Gingervitas, with Absolut® Citron vodka, dry vermouth and ginger ale.

Ingredients
1 shot Absolut® Citron vodka
1 shot dry vermouth
3 shots ginger ale

Instructions
Pour absolut citron and vermouth into an ice-filled shaker. Shake and pour into a cocktail glass. Add ginger ale, and serve.

Serving
Cocktail Glass
****

Girasole Cocktail recipe

Description
A delicious recipe for Girasole Cocktail, with Absolut® Mandrin vodka, orange juice, Cointreau® orange liqueur and Cynar® artichoke liqueur.

Ingredients
1 oz Absolut® Mandrin vodka
1 oz orange juice
1/2 oz Cointreau® orange liqueur
1/2 oz Cynar® artichoke liqueur

Instructions
Shake ingredients with ice and strain into a cocktail glass. Garnish with an orange slice, and serve.

Serving
Cocktail Glass
****

Gold Wizard recipe

Description
A delicious recipe for Gold Wizard, with Chardonnay white wine, banana liqueur, Absolut® vodka and cherry.

Ingredients
4 oz Chardonnay white wine
2 oz banana liqueur
1 oz Absolut® vodka
1 cherry

Instructions
Shake the Chardonnay, the banana liqueur and the vodka together in a cocktail shaker with 2 ice cubes for 30 seconds. Pour into a cocktail glass with a cherry at the bottom, and serve.

Serving
Cocktail Glass
****

Good Fortune recipe

Description
A delicious recipe for Good Fortune, with Absolut® Citron vodka, Alize® liqueur and lemonade.

Ingredients
1 1/4 oz Absolut® Citron vodka
3/4 oz Alize® liqueur
6 oz lemonade

Instructions
Shake and strain into an ice-filled hurricane glass. Garnish with a lemon wheel.

Serving
Hurricane Glass
****

Grand Hawaiian Screw recipe

Description
A delicious recipe for Grand Hawaiian Screw, with Absolut® vodka, Grand Marnier® orange liqueur, pineapple juice and orange juice.

Ingredients
1 oz Absolut® vodka
1/2 oz Grand Marnier® orange liqueur
fill with pineapple juice
1 splash orange juice

Instructions
Pour ingredients into a large rocks or old-fashioned glass filled with ice. Garnish a slice of orange or a pineapple wedge, and serve.

Serving
Highball Glass
****

Grape Ape #2 recipe

Description
A delicious recipe for Grape Ape #2, with Absolut® vodka, Malibu® coconut rum and grape juice.

Ingredients
1 oz Absolut® vodka
1 oz Malibu® coconut rum
4 oz grape juice

Instructions
Stir ingredients together in a highball glass filled with ice cubes, and serve.

Serving
Highball Glass
****

Green Cow #2 recipe

Description
A delicious recipe for Green Cow #2, with Absolut® vodka, Pisang Ambon® liqueur, milk and Sprite® soda.

Ingredients
4 cl Absolut® vodka
3 cl Pisang Ambon® liqueur
2 cl milk
fill with Sprite® soda

Instructions
Stir ingredients together and serve.

Serving
Old-Fashioned Glass
****

Green Creeper recipe

Description
A delicious recipe for Green Creeper, with Absolut® vodka, Midori® melon liqueur and Malibu® coconut rum.

Ingredients
3/4 oz Absolut® vodka
3/4 oz Midori® melon liqueur
3/4 oz Malibu® coconut rum

Instructions
Pour all ingredients over ice.

Serving
Highball Glass
****

Green Delight recipe

Description
A delicious recipe for Green Delight, with Absolut® vodka, Pisang Ambon® liqueur, Sprite® soda and orange juice.

Ingredients
2 cl Absolut® vodka
2 cl Pisang Ambon® liqueur
6 cl light Sprite® soda
6 cl orange juice

Instructions
Mix all the ingredients together, and serve cold.

Serving
Highball Glass
****

Green Froggy recipe

Description
A delicious recipe for Green Froggy, with Absolut® vodka and Mountain Dew® citrus soda.

Ingredients
2 shots Absolut® vodka
1 glass Mountain Dew® citrus soda

Instructions
Pour ingredients into an old-fashioned glass and stir.

Serving
Old-Fashioned Glass
****

Green Slime recipe

Description
A delicious recipe for Green Slime, with Absolut® vodka, Captain Morgan® Parrot Bay coconut rum, blueberry schnapps, Blue Curacao liqueur and orange juice.

Ingredients
1/2 oz Absolut® vodka
1/2 oz Captain Morgan® Parrot Bay coconut rum
1/2 oz blueberry schnapps
1/2 oz Blue Curacao liqueur
1 oz orange juice

Instructions
Shake with ice and strain into a lowball glass.

Serving
Old-Fashioned Glass
****

Greven recipe

Description
A delicious recipe for Greven, with Absolut® Citron vodka, Passoa® liqueur, Blue Curacao liqueur, orange juice and limes.

Ingredients
4 cl Absolut® Citron vodka
8 cl Passoa® liqueur
1 cl Blue Curacao liqueur
12 cl orange juice
2 dashes limes

Instructions
Pour vodka, passoa and orange juice over ice in the glass. Add the blue curacao and the lime. Do not stir.

Serving
Collins Glass
****

Grown-up Lemonade recipe

Description
A delicious recipe for Grown-up Lemonade, with Absolut® Citron vodka, triple sec, amaretto almond liqueur and lemonade.

Ingredients
1 oz Absolut® Citron vodka
1/2 oz triple sec
1/4 oz amaretto almond liqueur
lemonade

Instructions
Pour the vodka, triple sec and amaretto over ice in a cocktail glass. Fill glass with desired amount of lemonade. Garnish with lemon slice, and serve.

Serving
Cocktail Glass
****

G-Spot Martini recipe

Description
A delicious recipe for G-Spot Martini, with Absolut® Citron vodka, grapefruit juice, pineapple juice and Grand Marnier® orange liqueur.

Ingredients
2 oz Absolut® Citron vodka
1/2 oz grapefruit juice

1/2 oz pineapple juice
1 splash Grand Marnier® orange liqueur

Instructions
Shake ingredients with ice and pour into chilled martini glass. Garnish with one fresh rasberry, and serve.

Serving
Cocktail Glass
****

Gun Barrel recipe

Description
A delicious recipe for Gun Barrel, with Absolut® Kurant vodka, triple sec and cranberry juice.

Ingredients
1 1/2 oz Absolut® Kurant vodka
1/2 oz triple sec
1 splash cranberry juice

Instructions
Add vodka, triple sec and cranberry juice to a mixing glass, and mix well. Pour into a cocktail glass, and serve.

Serving
Cocktail Glass
****

H2O Martini recipe

Description
A delicious recipe for H2O Martini, with Hpnotiq® liqueur, Absolut® Citron vodka and 7-Up® soda.

Ingredients
3 oz Hpnotiq® liqueur
1 1/2 oz Absolut® Citron vodka
1 splash 7-Up® soda

Instructions
Shake and strain into a chilled martini glass rimmed with colored sugar. Garnish with a lemon slice, and serve.

Serving
Cocktail Glass
****

Haleakala Martini recipe

Description
A delicious recipe for Haleakala Martini, with Absolut® vodka, Chambord® raspberry liqueur and pineapple juice.

Ingredients
1 1/2 oz Absolut® vodka
1/2 oz Chambord® raspberry liqueur
2 oz pineapple juice

Instructions
Pour the Absolut vodka, Chambord raspberry liqueur and pineapple juice into a cocktail shaker half-filled with ice cubes. Shake well, strain into a chilled cocktail glass, and serve.

Serving
Cocktail Glass
****

Halfway Special recipe

Description
A delicious recipe for Halfway Special, with orange juice, Absolut® Citron vodka, Black Haus® blackberry schnapps, Malibu® coconut rum and grenadine syrup.

Ingredients
5 oz orange juice
1 oz Absolut® Citron vodka
1 oz Black Haus® blackberry schnapps
1 oz Malibu® coconut rum
2 dashes grenadine syrup

Instructions
Combine with ice, strain, and serve in a hollowed-out pineapple.
****

Hand Job recipe

Description
A delicious recipe for Hand Job, with Absolut® vodka, tequila, banana liqueur and Carolans® Irish cream.

Ingredients
1 oz Absolut® vodka
1 oz tequila
1 oz banana liqueur
1 oz Carolans® Irish cream

Instructions
Shake all ingredients in a cocktail shaker half-filled with ice cubes. Strain into a chilled cocktail glass, and serve.

Serving
Cocktail Glass
****

Hard Green Bricaki recipe

Description
A delicious recipe for Hard Green Bricaki, with Absolut® Citron vodka, Malibu® coconut rum, Midori® melon liqueur, lime juice, pineapple juice and lime.

Ingredients
1 oz Absolut® Citron vodka
1 oz Malibu® coconut rum
1 oz Midori® melon liqueur
1 dash lime juice
3 oz pineapple juice
1 slice lime

Instructions

Fill a glass with ice and add liquors. Add a dash of lime juice. Fill to top with pineapple juice. Shake well and serve. Garnish with a slice of lime and a cherry.

Serving
Hurricane Glass
****

Harlem World Seven recipe

Description
A delicious recipe for Harlem World Seven, with Absolut® vodka, Absolut® Kurant vodka, lemon juice, prune juice, black sambuca and gin.

Ingredients
3/4 oz Absolut® vodka
1/2 oz Absolut® Kurant vodka
1/4 tsp lemon juice
1 pint prune juice
1 1/2 qt black sambuca
fill with gin

Instructions
Mix over ice cubes, pour into a suitable glass and consume immediately.

NOTE: It might taste funny because of the prune juice but you should get an effect out of it.

Serving
Pitcher
****

Hawaiian Volcano recipe

Description
A delicious recipe for Hawaiian Volcano, with Absolut® vodka, Southern Comfort® peach liqueur, sloe gin, Grand Marnier® orange liqueur and orange juice.

Ingredients

2 oz Absolut® vodka
2 oz Southern Comfort® peach liqueur
2 oz sloe gin
2 oz Grand Marnier® orange liqueur
orange juice

Instructions
Shake with ice and strain into shot glasses.

Serving
Shot Glass
****

Hematoma recipe

Description
A delicious recipe for Hematoma, with Absolut® vodka, grape juice, orange juice, cranberry juice and Blue Curacao liqueur.

Ingredients
1 1/2 oz Absolut® vodka
2 1/2 oz grape juice
2 1/2 oz orange juice
1 oz cranberry juice
1/4 oz Blue Curacao liqueur

Instructions
Combine the Absolut vodka, grape juice, orange juice and cranberry juice in a cocktail shaker half-filled with ice cubes. Shake well and pour into a collins glass filled with crushed ice. Pour blue curacao in on the top, and serve.

Serving
Collins Glass
****

Honey Bunny recipe

Description
A delicious recipe for Honey Bunny, with Absolut® vodka, Blue Curacao liqueur, DeKuyper® Peachtree schnapps, sweet and sour mix, pear cider, 7-Up® soda and lemon juice.

Ingredients
2 oz Absolut® vodka
1 oz Blue Curacao liqueur
1 oz DeKuyper® Peachtree schnapps
2 oz sweet and sour mix
1/2 oz pear cider
1/2 oz 7-Up® soda
1/2 oz lemon juice

Instructions
Pour all ingredients into a highball glass 3/4 filled with ice cubes. Stir well, and serve.

Serving
Highball Glass
****

Hot Tub recipe

Description
A delicious recipe for Hot Tub, with Grand Marnier® orange liqueur, Absolut® vodka, Champagne, Chambord® raspberry liqueur and cranberry juice.

Ingredients
3/4 oz Grand Marnier® orange liqueur
3/4 oz Absolut® vodka
3/4 oz Champagne
3/4 oz Chambord® raspberry liqueur
4 oz cranberry juice

Instructions
Pour cranberry juice over ice in a tall glass. Add the Grand Marnier, Absolut, Champagne and Chambord. Garnish with a cherry, and serve.

Serving

Highball Glass
****

Hurlyburly recipe

Description
A delicious recipe for Hurlyburly, with Absolut® Citron vodka, Cointreau® orange liqueur, sweet and sour mix, orange juice and cranberry juice.

Ingredients
1 1/4 oz Absolut® Citron vodka
5/8 oz Cointreau® orange liqueur
1 oz sweet and sour mix
1/2 oz orange juice
1/2 oz cranberry juice

Instructions
Shake and strain into a chilled cocktail glass. Garnish with dried cranberries.

Serving
Cocktail Glass
****

Ice House Highball recipe

Description
A delicious recipe for Ice House Highball, with Absolut® Citron vodka, lemonade and white creme de menthe.

Ingredients
1 1/2 oz Absolut® Citron vodka
5 oz fresh lemonade
1 dash white creme de menthe

Instructions
Build the vodka and lemonade in a large pint glass filled with ice, and top with a dash of creme de menthe. Garnish with an edible orchid flower.

Serving
Beer Mug
****

Idaho Dimetapp recipe

Description
A delicious recipe for Idaho Dimetapp, with Absolut® vodka, Malibu® coconut rum and NuGrape® soda.

Ingredients
2 oz Absolut® vodka
2 oz Malibu® coconut rum
6 oz chilled NuGrape® soda

Instructions
Combine the vodka and rum in a cocktail shaker half-filled with ice cubes. Shake well and strain into a highball glass. Add the chilled grape soda and serve.

Serving
Highball Glass
****

Inferno recipe

Description
A delicious recipe for Inferno, with Absolut® Peppar vodka, Everclear® alcohol, Tabasco® sauce and salt.

Ingredients
1 part Absolut® Peppar vodka
1 part Everclear® alcohol
6 drops Tabasco® sauce
1 pinch salt

Instructions
Add tabasco sauce into the bottom of a shot glass, pour equal parts absolut peppar and everclear 190 then add salt. Set on fire and serve.

Serving
Shot Glass
****

Intercourse recipe

Description
A delicious recipe for Intercourse, with Absolut® vodka, orange juice, Hawaiian punch and Mountain Dew® citrus soda.

Ingredients
1 oz Absolut® vodka
2 oz orange juice
1/2 oz Hawaiian punch
1/2 oz Mountain Dew® citrus soda

Instructions
Pour the Absolut vodka and orange juice into a cocktail glass. Stir well. Top with equal amounts of Hawaiian fruit punch and mountain dew, and serve.

Serving
Cocktail Glass
****

Inverted Pyramid Martini recipe

Description
A delicious recipe for Inverted Pyramid Martini, with Absolut® Citron vodka, Absolut® Kurant vodka and Grand Marnier® orange liqueur.

Ingredients
1 1/4 oz Absolut® Citron vodka
1 1/4 oz Absolut® Kurant vodka
1 splash Grand Marnier® orange liqueur

Instructions
Shake all ingredients together in a cocktail shaker. Strain into a chilled martini glass and garnish with an orange twist.

Serving
Cocktail Glass
****

Inverted Traffic Light recipe

Description
A delicious recipe for Inverted Traffic Light, with peach schnapps, orange juice, grenadine syrup, Blue Curacao liqueur and Absolut® vodka.

Ingredients
1 oz peach schnapps
orange juice
1/2 oz grenadine syrup
1/2 oz Blue Curacao liqueur
1/2 oz Absolut® vodka

Instructions
Fill a cocktail glass with ice. Pour in peach schnapps, then add orange juice 3/4 to the top and shake. Slowly add and sink the grenadine to the bottom. In a mixer, mix the blue curacao with vodka and slowly strain that into the cocktail glass.

Serving
Cocktail Glass
****

Italian Ice #2 recipe

Description
A delicious recipe for Italian Ice #2, with Black Haus® blackberry schnapps, Absolut® Citron vodka and lemon juice.

Ingredients
1 oz Black Haus® blackberry schnapps
1 oz Absolut® Citron vodka
1 splash lemon juice

Instructions
Pour all ingredients into a cocktail shaker half-filled with ice cubes.

Shake well, strain into a shot glass, and serve.

Serving
Shot Glass
****

Italian Stallion #2 recipe

Description
A delicious recipe for Italian Stallion #2, with sambuca, orange juice and Absolut® Citron vodka.

Ingredients
1 oz sambuca
2 oz orange juice
1 oz Absolut® Citron vodka

Instructions
Pour sambuca into a cocktail shaker filled with ice. Add Absolut Citron and orange juice, and shake well. Strain into a chilled cocktail/martini glass, garnish with a twist of orange peel. (To rim the glass with lemon and sugar is optional.) Serve.

Serving
Cocktail Glass
****

Jacobs Haze recipe

Description
A delicious recipe for Jacobs Haze, with Jagermeister® herbal liqueur, Absolut® Kurant vodka, Red Bull® energy drink, kiwi and ice cubes.

Ingredients
2 cl Jagermeister® herbal liqueur
2 cl Absolut® Kurant vodka
1 can Red Bull® energy drink
1 slice kiwi
3 ice cubes

Instructions

Mix vodka, jagermeister and red bull in a glass. Add ice and a slice of kiwi.

Serving
Highball Glass
****

Jersey Shore Cherry Lemonade recipe

Description
A delicious recipe for Jersey Shore Cherry Lemonade, with Absolut® vodka, sweet and sour mix, sugar, Sprite® soda and grenadine syrup.

Ingredients
1 1/2 oz Absolut® vodka
1 1/4 oz sweet and sour mix
1 tsp sugar
fill with Sprite® soda
top with grenadine syrup

Instructions
Add sugar, vodka, and sour mix over ice and shake. Fill with sprite/7-up, and top with grenadine or cherry juice. Garnish with a cherry and lemon wedge.

Serving
Highball Glass
****

Joe Cassano recipe

Description
A delicious recipe for Joe Cassano, with Zima, Absolut® Citron vodka, gin, Bacardi® 151 rum and lemonade.

Ingredients
1 oz Zima
1/2 oz Absolut® Citron vodka
1/2 oz gin
1/3 oz Bacardi® 151 rum
1 1/2 oz lemonade

Instructions
Combine ingredients with 1 oz of crushed ice in a blender. Pour into a chilled cocktail glass, top with lemonade (to taste), and serve.

Serving
Cocktail Glass

****

Jogeir recipe

Description
A delicious recipe for Jogeir, with Absolut® Citron vodka, Hammer® lime vodka, orange juice and Galliano® herbal liqueur.

Ingredients
1 cl Absolut® Citron vodka
1 cl Hammer® lime vodka
1 cl orange juice
1 cl Galliano® herbal liqueur

Instructions
Mix lime vodka, absolut citron and juice together and put it in a shot glass. Add galliano right before serving. Shoot it.

Serving
Shot Glass

****

John Daly recipe

Description
A delicious recipe for John Daly, with Absolut® Citron vodka, triple sec, lemonade, iced tea and ice cubes.

Ingredients
1 1/4 oz Absolut® Citron vodka
1/4 oz triple sec
fill with 1/2 lemonade
fill with 1/2 iced tea
ice cubes

Instructions
Fill a collins glass with ice. Add absolute citron and triple sec. Fill glass with equal parts lemonade/iced tea. Garnish with a lemon wedge.

Serving
Collins Glass
****

John Rocker recipe

Description
A delicious recipe for John Rocker, with Absolut® vodka, peach schnapps and grape juice.

Ingredients
2 oz Absolut® vodka
1 1/2 oz peach schnapps
4 1/2 oz grape juice

Instructions
Pour all ingredients into a collins glass filled with ice cubes. Garnish with an orange wedge, and serve.

Serving
Collins Glass
****

Johnny Bravo recipe

Description
A delicious recipe for Johnny Bravo, with Absolut® vodka, peach schnapps, DeKuyper® Watermelon Pucker schnapps, Blue Curacao liqueur and cranberry juice.

Ingredients
1 oz Absolut® vodka
1 oz peach schnapps
1 oz DeKuyper® Watermelon Pucker schnapps
1 oz Blue Curacao liqueur
2 oz cranberry juice

Instructions
Pour the Absolut vodka, peach schnapps, DeKuyper Watermelon Pucker schnapps and blue curacao into a highball glass filled with ice cubes. Add the cranberry juice, and serve.

Serving
Highball Glass
****

Johnny Rev recipe

Description
A delicious recipe for Johnny Rev, with Absolut® Mandrin vodka, tonic water, lime and mandarin.

Ingredients
3 oz Absolut® Mandrin vodka
4 oz tonic water
1 lime wedge
1 mandarin slice

Instructions
Pour vodka and tonic water over a fair amount of ice in a highball glass. Squeeze juices from lime and mandarin slices and garnish. Make sure to use ripe, sweet limes to counterbalance the tonic water.

Serving
Highball Glass
****

Joy Ride recipe

Description
A delicious recipe for Joy Ride, with Absolut® Citron vodka, Campari® bitters, sweet and sour mix, lemons, sugar and soda water.

Ingredients
1 1/4 oz Absolut® Citron vodka
3/4 oz Campari® bitters
3 oz sweet and sour mix

2 lemons wedges
1 tbsp sugar
soda water

Instructions
Muddle lemon and sugar in a mixing glass. Add ice, absolut citron, campari and sweet and sour. Shake well and dump into a hurricane glass. Spritz with soda.

Serving
Hurricane Glass
****

Juicy Guiness Premier recipe

Description
A delicious recipe for Juicy Guiness Premier, with Blue Curacao liqueur, Taboo®, Absolut® vodka, Guinness® stout and Carling® Premier lager.

Ingredients
1 shot Blue Curacao liqueur
1 shot Taboo®
1 shot Absolut® vodka
1/2 pint Guinness® stout
fill with Carling® Premier lager

Instructions
Mix in the shots of blue curacao, taboo and vodka. Add the guinness to the spirits up to 3cm below the rim of the pint glass. Allow the guinness to settle before adding the carling premier. Allow to settle again before consuming.

Serving
Beer Mug
****

Kamakazie #2 recipe

Description
A delicious recipe for Kamakazie #2, with Absolut® vodka, Cointreau® orange liqueur and lime.

Ingredients
1 1/2 oz Absolut® vodka
1/2 oz Cointreau® orange liqueur
1 lime wedge

Instructions
Pour absolut and cointreau over ice in an old-fashioned glass. Squeeze and drop in lime wedge to taste.

Serving
Old-Fashioned Glass
****

Krypto Kami recipe

Description
A delicious recipe for Krypto Kami, with Absolut® Kurant vodka, Midori® melon liqueur, peach schnapps, pineapple juice and sweet and sour mix.

Ingredients
1/2 oz Absolut® Kurant vodka
1/2 oz Midori® melon liqueur
1/2 oz peach schnapps
1/2 oz pineapple juice
1/2 oz sweet and sour mix

Instructions
Shake ingredients in a mixing tin filled with ice. Strain into a highball glass.

Serving
Highball Glass
****

Kurant Collins recipe

Description
A delicious recipe for Kurant Collins, with Absolut® Kurant vodka, lemon juice, powdered sugar and club soda.

Ingredients
2 oz Absolut® Kurant vodka
1 oz lemon juice
1 tsp powdered sugar
3 oz club soda

Instructions
In a shaker half-filled with ice cubes, combine the absolut kurant, lemon juice, and sugar. Shake well. Strain into a collins glass almost filled with ice cubes. Add the club soda.

Serving
Collins Glass
****

Kurant recipe

Description
A delicious recipe for Kurant, with Absolut® Kurant vodka, Schweppes® Russian tonic water and ice cubes.

Ingredients
4 cl Absolut® Kurant vodka
fill with Schweppes® Russian tonic water
ice cubes

Instructions
Put some ice cubes into a highball glass. Pour absolut kurant into the glass and fill up with schweppes russian. Serve with a straw.

Serving
Highball Glass
****

Kurant Shot recipe

Description
A delicious recipe for Kurant Shot, with Absolut® Kurant vodka and Sprite® soda.

Ingredients
2 cl Absolut® Kurant vodka
fill with Sprite® soda

Instructions
Pour absolut kurant into a glass and fill up with sprite and ice.
****

Kurant Tea recipe

Description
A delicious recipe for Kurant Tea, with Absolut® Kurant vodka, Turkish apple tea and sugar.

Ingredients
4 cl Absolut® Kurant vodka
Turkish apple tea
1 tsp sugar

Instructions
Pour absolut kurant into a comfortably big tea-cup. Add hot/very warm apple tea and, if you like, some sugar.

Serving
Champagne Flute
****

Lake George Iced Tea recipe

Description
A delicious recipe for Lake George Iced Tea, with Jose Cuervo® Especial gold tequila, Bacardi® white rum, Absolut® vodka, Beefeater® gin, triple sec, pineapple juice and Pepsi® cola. Also lists similar drink recipes

Ingredients
1/2 oz Jose Cuervo® Especial gold tequila
1/2 oz Bacardi® white rum
1/2 oz Absolut® vodka
1/2 oz Beefeater® gin
1/2 oz triple sec

1 oz pineapple juice
Pepsi® cola

Instructions
Shake all ingredients (except cola), and pour into a highball glass. Fill with pepsi, stir gently, and serve.

Serving
Highball Glass
****

Lakeside Lemonade recipe

Description
A delicious recipe for Lakeside Lemonade, with Absolut® Citron vodka, triple sec, sweet and sour mix, lemon-lime soda and cranberry juice.

Ingredients
1 1/2 oz Absolut® Citron vodka
1/2 oz triple sec
4 1/2 oz sweet and sour mix
1 splash lemon-lime soda
1 splash cranberry juice

Instructions
Pour the Absolut Citron and triple sec into a highball glass filled with ice cubes. Almost fill with sweet and sour mix, and add a splash of lemon-lime soda and splash of cranberry juice. Garnish with a slice of lemon, and serve.

Serving
Highball Glass
****

Lava Lamp recipe

Description
A delicious recipe for Lava Lamp, with Absolut® Citron vodka, apple juice and grenadine syrup.

Ingredients
2 oz Absolut® Citron vodka
6 oz apple juice
3 ml grenadine syrup

Instructions
Pour grenadine over ice in a highball glass. Add absolut citron, and fill with apple juice.

Serving
Highball Glass
****

Lemon Drop #2 recipe

Description
A delicious recipe for Lemon Drop #2, with Absolut® Citron vodka, lemon and sugar.

Ingredients
1 shot Absolut® Citron vodka
1 slice lemon
1 tsp sugar

Instructions
Place sugar on lemon, place in mouth and take shot, then bite down on lemon.

Serving
Shot Glass
****

Lemon Drop #3 recipe

Description
A delicious recipe for Lemon Drop #3, with Absolut® Citron vodka, sweet and sour mix, lemon and sugar.

Ingredients
1/2 shot Absolut® Citron vodka
1/2 shot sweet and sour mix
1 slice lemon
1/2 tsp sugar

Instructions
Mix equal parts absolut citron and sweet and sour mix over ice then strain into a shot glass. Sprinkle sugar on lemon slice. Drink shot, then suck the lemon.

Serving
Shot Glass
****

Lemon Drop #5 recipe

Description
A delicious recipe for Lemon Drop #5, with Absolut® Citron vodka, margarita mix, triple sec, lemons and sugar.

Ingredients
2 1/2 oz Absolut® Citron vodka
2 oz margarita mix
2 tbsp triple sec
juice of 1 lemons
2 packages sugar

Instructions
Pour over cracked ice, and strain into a cocktail glass with sugar around its rim.

Serving
Cocktail Glass
****

Lemon Drop #6 recipe

Description
A delicious recipe for Lemon Drop #6, with Absolut® vodka,

Cointreau® orange liqueur, lemon, ice and sugar.

Ingredients
1 1/2 shots Absolut® vodka
1 1/2 shots Cointreau® orange liqueur
1 lemon wedge
ice
sugar

Instructions
Put the vodka and cointreau into a shaker. Squeeze the lemon juice into the shaker. Put a good amount of ice in the shaker, close and shake until cold.

Moisten the rim of a cocktail glass and then dip the rim in the sugar. Strain the contents of the shaker into the glass. Garnish with lemon zest for a decorative touch.

Serving
Cocktail Glass
****

Lemon Drop Martini #2 recipe

Description
A delicious recipe for Lemon Drop Martini #2, with Absolut® Citron vodka, limoncello lemon liqueur, sweet and sour mix, lemon juice and sugar.

Ingredients
1 - 1 1/2 oz Absolut® Citron vodka
1 - 1 1/2 oz limoncello lemon liqueur
2 oz sweet and sour mix
1 - 1 1/2 oz fresh lemon juice
1 tsp sugar

Instructions
Combine ingredients in a cocktail shaker half-filled with ice cubes; shake well. Swirl half a lemon around the rim of a margarita glass and dip in sugar. Pour the contents of the cocktail shaker into the glass, and serve.

Serving
Margarita Glass
****

Lemon Joe recipe

Description
A delicious recipe for Lemon Joe, with Bacardi® Limon rum, Absolut® Citron vodka and 7-Up® soda.

Ingredients
1 oz Bacardi® Limon rum
1 oz Absolut® Citron vodka
4 oz 7-Up® soda

Instructions
Pour the Bacardi Limon rum and Absolut Citron vodka into a highball glass filled with ice cubes. Stir well, garnish with a slice of lemon, and serve.

Serving
Highball Glass
****

Lemon Shot recipe

Description
A delicious recipe for Lemon Shot, with Galliano® herbal liqueur, Absolut® Citron vodka, lemon, sugar and Bacardi® 151 rum.

Ingredients
1/2 oz Galliano® herbal liqueur
1/2 oz Absolut® Citron vodka
1 lemon wedge
sugar
Bacardi® 151 rum

Instructions
Mix galliano and absolut citron in a shot glass, lay lemon wedge

sprinkled with sugar over glass and pour rum over the wedge and glass. Ignite rum and allow to burn for a moment. Extinguish, shoot quickly, and suck on the lemon.

If it is done correctly, this will taste like a shot of sweet lemonade.

Serving
Shot Glass
****

Lemon Twist recipe

Description
A delicious recipe for Lemon Twist, with Absolut® Citron vodka and dry vermouth.

Ingredients
3 oz Absolut® Citron vodka
1/2 oz dry vermouth

Instructions
Shake the vodka and vermouth with cracked ice in a cocktail shaker. Strain into a chilled cocktail glass. Garnish with a lemon twist, and serve.

Serving
Cocktail Glass
****

Lemon Twister recipe

Description
A delicious recipe for Lemon Twister, with Absolut® Citron vodka, lemonade and lemon.

Ingredients
2 1/2 oz Absolut® Citron vodka
fill with lemonade
1 slice lemon

Instructions
Shake together, stirring bruises the vodka.

Serving
Highball Glass
****

Lemonade Bomb recipe

Description
A delicious recipe for Lemonade Bomb, with lemonade, Absolut® vodka and beer.

Ingredients
1 can lemonade concentrate
3 cups Absolut® vodka
7 cans beer

Instructions
Follow the instructions on the can of lemonade concentrate, but substitute the vodka for water. Mix well and add beer.

Serving
Pitcher
****

Lick and a Promise recipe

Description
A delicious recipe for Lick and a Promise, with Absolut® Mandrin vodka, Cointreau® orange liqueur, cranberry juice, orange juice and Midori® melon liqueur.

Ingredients
1 1/2 oz Absolut® Mandrin vodka
3/4 oz Cointreau® orange liqueur
2 oz cranberry juice
1 splash orange juice
1 dash Midori® melon liqueur

Instructions
Pour the Absolut vodka, Cointreau, cranberry juice and orange juice into a highball glass filled with ice cubes. Shake well. Drizzle Midori melon

liqueur on top, and serve.

Serving
Highball Glass
****

Liquid Cocaine #2 recipe

Description
A delicious recipe for Liquid Cocaine #2, with Grand Marnier® orange liqueur, Southern Comfort® peach liqueur, Absolut® vodka, amaretto almond liqueur and pineapple juice.

Ingredients
1/4 shot Grand Marnier® orange liqueur
1/4 shot Southern Comfort® peach liqueur
1/4 shot Absolut® vodka
1/4 shot amaretto almond liqueur
1 splash pineapple juice

Instructions
Combine 4 alcohols and pineapple juice into a cocktail mixer with ice. Shake well. Strain into a shot glass and serve.

Serving
Shot Glass
****

Liquid Desert recipe

Description
A delicious recipe for Liquid Desert, with Absolut® vodka, Midori® melon liqueur, water and Mello Yello® citrus soda.

Ingredients
1/2 oz Absolut® vodka
2 oz Midori® melon liqueur
1 oz water
2 oz Mello Yello® citrus soda

Instructions

Pour ingredients over ice cubes in an old-fashioned glass, stir, and serve.

Serving
Old-Fashioned Glass
****

Long Iver Iced Tea recipe

Description
A delicious recipe for Long Iver Iced Tea, with Malibu® coconut rum, Absolut® vodka, Tanqueray® gin, tequila, triple sec, sweet and sour mix, Coca-Cola® and lemon.

Ingredients
1/4 oz Malibu® coconut rum
1/4 oz Absolut® vodka
1/4 oz Tanqueray® gin
1/4 oz tequila
1/4 oz triple sec
sweet and sour mix
Coca-Cola®
1 lemon wedge

Instructions
Pour liquor over ice. Fill 3/4 full with sour mix. Shake. Top with cola and add a lemon wedge.

Serving
Collins Glass
****

Loopy Lemonade recipe

Description
A delicious recipe for Loopy Lemonade, with Absolut® Citron vodka, lemons, granulated sugar, 7-Up® soda, sweet and sour mix and ice cubes.

Ingredients
2 oz Absolut® Citron vodka
2 squeezed lemons wedges

3 packages granulated sugar
7-Up® soda
fill with sweet and sour mix
ice cubes

Instructions
Fill a pint glass with ice. Add absolut citron, squeeze two lemon wedges and add three packages of sugar. Fill remainder of glass with 7-up and sweet and sour mix.

Serving
Beer Mug
****

Love Potion recipe

Description
A delicious recipe for Love Potion, with Absolut® vodka, amaretto almond liqueur, peach schnapps, orange juice, cranberry juice and ice cubes.

Ingredients
1 oz Absolut® vodka
1 oz amaretto almond liqueur
1 oz peach schnapps
1 oz orange juice
1 oz cranberry juice
ice cubes

Instructions
Pour ingredients into a shaker with ice, shake and serve on the rocks.

Serving
Shot Glass
****

Lucky Double recipe

Description
A delicious recipe for Lucky Double, with lemon, triple sec and Absolut® Mandrin vodka.

Ingredients
1/2 lemon
1/2 oz triple sec
2 oz Absolut® Mandrin vodka

Instructions
Slice the lemon half further into four quarters, and drop into to a mixing glass. Add triple sec and muddle well. Add absolut mandrin and ice, shake well, and pour out into an old-fashioned glass. Serve.

Serving
Old-Fashioned Glass
****

Ludvika Walker recipe

Description
A delicious recipe for Ludvika Walker, with Absolut® Kurant vodka and apple cider.

Ingredients
4 cl Absolut® Kurant vodka
5 cl apple cider

Instructions
Mix and add some ice.

Serving
Highball Glass
****

Lyndy recipe

Description
A delicious recipe for Lyndy, with Absolut® Mandrin vodka and cranberry juice.

Ingredients
50 ml Absolut® Mandrin vodka
1 - 2 cups cranberry juice

Instructions
Shake with ice and serve.

Serving
Collins Glass
****

M.V.P. recipe

Description
A delicious recipe for M.V.P., with Absolut® vodka, Midori® melon liqueur, Malibu® coconut rum and pineapple juice.

Ingredients
2 oz Absolut® vodka
1 oz Midori® melon liqueur
1 oz Malibu® coconut rum
fill with pineapple juice

Instructions
Pour vodka, midori, and malibu into an ice-filled hurricane glass. Fill with pineapple juice. Stir or shake.

Serving
Hurricane Glass
****

Magic Mountain Dew recipe

Description
A delicious recipe for Magic Mountain Dew, with Absolut® Citron vodka, triple sec and Mountain Dew® citrus soda.

Ingredients
1 1/2 oz Absolut® Citron vodka
1 1/2 oz triple sec
3 oz Mountain Dew® citrus soda

Instructions
Pour the Absolut Citron vodka and triple sec into a cocktail shaker half-

filled with ice cubes. Shake well, and strain into a highball glass filled with ice cubes. Top with mountain dew, stir briefly and serve.

Serving
Highball Glass
****

Magic Punch recipe

Description
A delicious recipe for Magic Punch, with Absolut® vodka, guava juice, papaya juice and mango juice.

Ingredients
4 oz Absolut® vodka
1 oz guava juice
1 oz papaya juice
1 oz mango juice

Instructions
Add ingredients to an ice-filled collins glass and shake.

Serving
Collins Glass
****

Malibu Paradise recipe

Description
A delicious recipe for Malibu Paradise, with Malibu® coconut rum, Absolut® vodka, cranberry juice and pineapple juice.

Ingredients
1 oz Malibu® coconut rum
1/2 oz Absolut® vodka
1 oz cranberry juice
1/2 oz pineapple juice

Instructions
Pour the Malibu coconut rum, Absolut vodka, cranberry and pineapple juice into a cocktail shaker half-filled with ice cubes. Shake well, pour

into a chilled cocktail glass, and serve.

Serving
Cocktail Glass
****

Malibu Smash recipe

Description
A delicious recipe for Malibu Smash, with Absolut® vodka, peach schnapps, Malibu® coconut rum, orange juice and grenadine syrup.

Ingredients
1 oz Absolut® vodka
1 oz peach schnapps
1 oz Malibu® coconut rum
orange juice
grenadine syrup

Instructions
Pour ingredients into a collins glass with ice, mix, and serve.

Serving
Collins Glass
****

Mandarin Crush recipe

Description
A delicious recipe for Mandarin Crush, with Absolut® Mandrin vodka and orange soda.

Ingredients
1 oz Absolut® Mandrin vodka
orange soda

Instructions
Add absolut mandrin to an ice-filled highball glass. Fill with orange soda.

Serving

Highball Glass
****

Mandarin Delight recipe

Description
A delicious recipe for Mandarin Delight, with Absolut® Mandrin vodka, tonic water and lime.

Ingredients
1 1/2 oz Absolut® Mandrin vodka
tonic water
1 lime wedge

Instructions
Pour absolut mandrin into a glass over ice. Fill with tonic water. Squeeze and drop the wedge of lime or orange into the drink. Stir, and serve.

Serving
Cocktail Glass
****

Mandarin Dream recipe

Description
A delicious recipe for Mandarin Dream, with Absolut® Mandrin vodka, orange juice, cranberry juice and orange.

Ingredients
1 3/4 oz Absolut® Mandrin vodka
1 splash orange juice
1 splash cranberry juice
1 slice orange

Instructions
Pour vodka and splash juices in a shaker with ice. Shake vigorously so when poured, a thin layer of ice crystals is visible. Strain into a cocktail glass and garnish with an orange slice.

Serving

Cocktail Glass
****

Mandarin Split recipe

Description
A delicious recipe for Mandarin Split, with Absolut® Mandrin vodka, strawberry schnapps, creme de bananes, grenadine syrup, Sprite® soda and pineapple juice.

Ingredients
1 oz Absolut® Mandrin vodka
1 oz strawberry schnapps
1/2 oz creme de bananes
1 splash grenadine syrup
1 part Sprite® soda
1 part pineapple juice

Instructions
Shake once, and strain into a collins glass.

Serving
Collins Glass
****

Mandarin Sunrise recipe

Description
A delicious recipe for Mandarin Sunrise, with Absolut® Mandrin vodka, pineapple juice, orange juice, peach schnapps, 7-Up® soda, grenadine syrup and lime.

Ingredients
1 1/2 oz Absolut® Mandrin vodka
4 oz pineapple juice
2 oz orange juice
1 oz peach schnapps
fill with 7-Up® soda
3/4 oz grenadine syrup
1 twist lime peel

Instructions
Combine absolut mandrin, peach schnapps and juices in a shaker with ice. Pour into a collins glass, fill with 7-up and stir. Sink the grenadine and garnish with a twist of lime.

Serving
Collins Glass
****

Mandrin Cherry Smash recipe

Description
A delicious recipe for Mandrin Cherry Smash, with lemon, cherry brandy and Absolut® Mandrin vodka.

Ingredients
1/2 lemon
3/4 oz cherry brandy
1 1/2 oz Absolut® Mandrin vodka

Instructions
Cut the lemon half into four quarters. Muddle with the cherry brandy in the bottom of a mixing glass. Add vodka and ice, and shake well. Pour into an old-fashioned glass, and serve.

Serving
Old-Fashioned Glass
****

Maria-Rocker recipe

Description
A delicious recipe for Maria-Rocker, with DeKuyper® Peachtree schnapps, Passoa® liqueur, Absolut® vodka, lime juice, cranberry juice and Sprite® soda.

Ingredients
1 oz DeKuyper® Peachtree schnapps
1 oz Passoa® liqueur
1 oz Absolut® vodka
1 splash fresh lime juice

1 splash cranberry juice
3 - 5 oz Sprite® soda

Instructions
Pour the DeKuyper Peachtree peach schnapps, passoa and Absolut vodka into a tall glass filled with ice cubes. Add the lime juice, and fill with Sprite. Add cranberry juice for color. Garnish with a slice of lime, and serve.
****

Martina Mandarina recipe

Description
A delicious recipe for Martina Mandarina, with Absolut® Mandrin vodka, cranberry juice and Grand Marnier® orange liqueur.

Ingredients
1 part Absolut® Mandrin vodka
2 parts cranberry juice
1 splash Grand Marnier® orange liqueur

Instructions
Pour juice, vodka and a splash of grand marnier in a shaker. Add ice, shake and strain into a cocktail glass. Garnish with a orange peel curl.

Serving
Cocktail Glass
****

Martini Dominikanis recipe

Description
A delicious recipe for Martini Dominikanis, with Absolut® Mandrin vodka, limoncello lemon liqueur and pineapple juice.

Ingredients
1 1/2 oz Absolut® Mandrin vodka
1/2 oz limoncello lemon liqueur
1 1/2 oz pineapple juice

Instructions

Shake ingredients with ice and strain into a chilled martini or cocktail glass. Garnish with a lemon, and serve.

Serving
Cocktail Glass
****

Mazerati recipe

Description
A delicious recipe for Mazerati, with Absolut® Citron vodka, cranberry juice and 7-Up® soda.

Ingredients
3/4 oz Absolut® Citron vodka
cranberry juice
7-Up® soda

Instructions
Pour the absolut citron into a highball glass, balance with cranberry juice and top with a little 7-up. Garnish with a lime slice.

Serving
Highball Glass
****

Mean Green Machine recipe

Description
A delicious recipe for Mean Green Machine, with Midori® melon liqueur, triple sec, Absolut® vodka and lime juice.

Ingredients
1 oz Midori® melon liqueur
1 oz triple sec
1 oz Absolut® vodka
1 oz lime juice

Instructions
Shake well with ice and strain into a highball glass.

Serving
Highball Glass
****

Melon Martini recipe

Description
A delicious recipe for Melon Martini, with melons, honey syrup, maraschino liqueur, lime juice and Absolut® Citron vodka.

Ingredients
1/2 cup chopped melons
1 oz honey syrup
1 oz maraschino liqueur
1 oz fresh lime juice
1 1/2 oz Absolut® Citron vodka

Instructions
Muddle the melon, honey syrup, maraschino liqueur and lime juice together in a large mixing glass. Add vodka and ice. Shake and strain into a chilled cocktail glass, garnish with a sprig of mint, and serve.

Serving
Cocktail Glass
****

Meloncholy Baby recipe

Description
A delicious recipe for Meloncholy Baby, with Absolut® Citron vodka, lemon juice, simple syrup, cantaloupe melons and water.

Ingredients
1 1/2 oz Absolut® Citron vodka
3/4 oz fresh lemon juice
2 oz simple syrup
1/2 cup chopped cantaloupe melons
3 oz water

Instructions
Blend all ingredients with crushed ice and pour into a collins glass.

Garnish with flamed orange peel, and serve.

Serving
Collins Glass
****

Merry Christmas recipe

Description
A delicious recipe for Merry Christmas, with raspberry vodka, cranberry juice, Absolut® vodka and Sprite® soda.

Ingredients
1 bottle raspberry vodka
6 cans cranberry juice
1/2 bottle Absolut® vodka
1 can Sprite® soda

Instructions
Pour all ingredients (chilled beforehand) into a large container or punch bowl, preferably on top of another similar container filled with ice. Allow to chill. Serve in punch cups or tall glasses.

Serving
Punch Bowl
****

Metropolitan #2 recipe

Description
A delicious recipe for Metropolitan #2, with Absolut® Citron vodka, Chambord® raspberry liqueur, lime juice and Ocean Spray® cranberry juice.

Ingredients
1 oz Absolut® Citron vodka
1 oz Chambord® raspberry liqueur
2 oz fresh lime juice
1 oz Ocean Spray® cranberry juice

Instructions
Build ingredients in a cocktail shaker half-filled with ice cubes. Shake and strain carefully into a sugar-rimmed 10-oz cocktail glass so as not to knock sugar off rim. Garnish with a large lemon twist, and serve.

Serving
Cocktail Glass
****

Miami Hurricane recipe

Description
A delicious recipe for Miami Hurricane, with Absolut® Kurant vodka, cranberry juice, orange juice and pineapple juice.

Ingredients
1 1/2 oz Absolut® Kurant vodka
2 parts cranberry juice
1 part orange juice
1 part pineapple juice

Instructions
Mix with ice cubes in a hurricane glass.

Serving
Hurricane Glass
****

Midori Hack recipe

Description
A delicious recipe for Midori Hack, with Midori® melon liqueur, Absolut® Citron vodka, sweet and sour mix and pineapple juice.

Ingredients
2 oz Midori® melon liqueur
1/2 oz Absolut® Citron vodka
4 oz sweet and sour mix
1 splash pineapple juice

Instructions
Shake midori, vodka, and sweet and sour over ice in a tin. Prepare a large rocks glass by juicing lime garnish into the glass half filled with ice. Strain in the chilled cocktail, add a splash of pineapple juice (upto half an ounce), and serve.

Serving
Old-Fashioned Glass

****

Miss Pastore recipe

Description
A delicious recipe for Miss Pastore, with Absolut® vodka, Campari® bitters, orange juice, Angostura® bitters, superfine sugar and lemon juice.

Ingredients
3 1/3 oz Absolut® vodka
2/3 oz Campari® bitters
5 oz red orange juice
2 drops Angostura® bitters
1 tbsp superfine sugar
1 oz fresh lemon juice

Instructions
Pour the Absolut vodka, Campari bitters, Angostura bitters, orange juice, superfine sugar and lemon juice into a highball glass rimmed with sugar and lemon. Stir vigorously, and serve.

Serving
Highball Glass

****

Missle Pop recipe

Description
A delicious recipe for Missle Pop, with Absolut® vodka, pineapple juice, fruit punch and orange juice.

Ingredients

2 1/2 oz Absolut® vodka
2 splashes pineapple juice
3 splashes fruit punch
fill with orange juice

Instructions
Pour vodka, pineapple juice and fruit punch into an ice-filled glass. Fill with orange juice, and serve.

Serving
Highball Glass
****

Mogadon recipe

Description
A delicious recipe for Mogadon, with Absolut® Citron vodka, 7-Up® soda and fruit juice.

Ingredients
1 oz Absolut® Citron vodka
fill with 7-Up® soda
1 splash fruit juice

Instructions
Pour absolut citron into a highball glass filled with ice cubes. Fill with 7-up, add a splash of fruit juice, and stir.

Serving
Highball Glass
****

Moilanen recipe

Description
A delicious recipe for Moilanen, with Absolut® Citron vodka, Schweppes® lemon soda and lemon.

Ingredients
1 part Absolut® Citron vodka
2 parts Schweppes® lemon soda

1 lemon

Instructions
1. Slice half a lemon into small slices. Extract the juice from the other half.

2. Add ice to a beer mug, and pour in the lemon juice. Fill the rest of the glass with vodka and schweppes, at a ratio of 1:2 respectively. Blend briefly.

Serving
Beer Mug
****

Mona-Lisa recipe

Description
A delicious recipe for Mona-Lisa, with Absolut® vodka and lemon soda.

Ingredients
1 part Absolut® vodka
1 part lemon soda

Instructions
Stir ingredients and pour into a highball glass.

Serving
Highball Glass
****

Mongolian Motherfucker recipe

Description
A delicious recipe for Mongolian Motherfucker, with Absolut® vodka, Kahlua® coffee liqueur, melon liqueur, creme de bananes, Southern Comfort® peach liqueur, sweet and sour mix, Sprite® soda and grenadine syrup. Also lists

Ingredients

1 part Absolut® vodka
1 part Kahlua® coffee liqueur
1 part melon liqueur
1 part creme de bananes
1 part Southern Comfort® peach liqueur
1 splash sweet and sour mix
1 splash Sprite® soda
1 squirt grenadine syrup

Instructions
Pour ingredients, in order, over ice. Shake, and serve.

Serving
Collins Glass
****

Naked Navel recipe

Description
A delicious recipe for Naked Navel, with Absolut® vodka and peach schnapps.

Ingredients
1 oz Absolut® vodka
1/2 oz peach schnapps

Instructions
Both vodka and schnapps should be kept in the freezer prior to making. Pour vodka into a shot glass, and add the schnapps, forming a ball in the bottom of the glass.

Serving
Shot Glass
****

Nestle recipe

Description
A delicious recipe for Nestle, with Absolut® Peppar vodka and Midori® melon liqueur.

Ingredients
3 cl Absolut® Peppar vodka
3 cl Midori® melon liqueur

Instructions
Combine in a shot glass and serve.

Serving
Shot Glass
****

New York Lemonade recipe

Description
A delicious recipe for New York Lemonade, with Absolut® Citron vodka, Grand Marnier® orange liqueur, lemon juice and club soda.

Ingredients
2 oz Absolut® Citron vodka
1 oz Grand Marnier® orange liqueur
2 oz lemon juice
1 oz club soda

Instructions
Stir and strain into a chilled cocktail glass with a frosted rim (lemon and sugar).

Serving
Cocktail Glass
****

Nickel Alloy recipe

Description
A delicious recipe for Nickel Alloy, with Absolut® Kurant vodka, Cointreau® orange liqueur, orange juice and 7-Up® soda.

Ingredients
1 1/3 oz Absolut® Kurant vodka
2/3 oz Cointreau® orange liqueur
2 oz orange juice

6 oz cold 7-Up® soda

Instructions
Pour the Absolut Kurant, Cointreau and orange juice into a cocktail shaker half-filled with ice cubes. Shake well, and strain into a highball glass. Fill with cold 7-up, and serve.

Serving
Highball Glass
****

Nickel recipe

Description
A delicious recipe for Nickel, with Absolut® Kurant vodka, Midori® melon liqueur, orange juice and 7-Up® soda.

Ingredients
1 1/3 oz Absolut® Kurant vodka
2/3 oz Midori® melon liqueur
2 oz orange juice
6 oz cold 7-Up® soda

Instructions
Pour the Absolut Kurant, Midori melon liqueur and orange juice into a cocktail shaker half-filled with ice cubes. Shake well, and strain into a highball glass. Fill with cold 7-up, and serve.

Serving
Highball Glass
****

Nicolalas recipe

Description
A delicious recipe for Nicolalas, with Absolut® Mandrin vodka, Passoa® liqueur and orange juice.

Ingredients
4 cl Absolut® Mandrin vodka
2 cl Passoa® liqueur

orange juice

Instructions
Mix absolut mandrin and passoa in a highball glass. Add ice and fill with orange juice.

Serving
Highball Glass
****

Northern Lights recipe

Description
A delicious recipe for Northern Lights, with Absolut® vodka, raspberry liqueur and orange-pineapple juice.

Ingredients
1 oz Absolut® vodka
2 oz raspberry liqueur
3 oz orange-pineapple juice

Instructions
Pour the Absolut vodka, raspberry liqueur and orange-pineapple juice into a highball glass filled with ice cubes. Stir well, and serve.

Serving
Highball Glass
****

Nuclear Slush recipe

Description
A delicious recipe for Nuclear Slush, with Absolut® Citron vodka, Bacardi® Limon rum, Midori® melon liqueur, Blue Curacao liqueur and sweet and sour mix.

Ingredients
3/4 oz Absolut® Citron vodka
3/4 oz Bacardi® Limon rum
1/2 oz Midori® melon liqueur
1/2 oz Blue Curacao liqueur

sweet and sour mix

Instructions
Fill a blender about 3/4 with crushed ice and add liqueurs. Mix and add the sour mix until the mixture funnels in the blender. The final result should be thick. Add more ice if necessary. Pour into a hurricane glass, and serve.

Serving
Hurricane Glass
****

Nuclear Waste #2 recipe

Description
A delicious recipe for Nuclear Waste #2, with Absolut® vodka, Kahlua® coffee liqueur, amaretto almond liqueur, root beer schnapps, dark creme de cacao and cream.

Ingredients
1/2 oz Absolut® vodka
1/2 oz Kahlua® coffee liqueur
1/2 oz amaretto almond liqueur
1/2 oz root beer schnapps
1/2 oz dark creme de cacao
fill with cream

Instructions
Shake well and serve in a highball glass.

Serving
Highball Glass
****

Nurse recipe

Description
A delicious recipe for Nurse, with Absolut® vodka, Licor 43® liqueur and root beer.

Ingredients

10 cl Absolut® vodka
5 cl Licor 43® liqueur
root beer

Instructions
Pour vodka and licor 43 over 2 - 3 ice cubes in a highball glass. Stir and fill with with root beer. Serve with a straw.

Serving
Highball Glass
****

NyQuil recipe

Description
A delicious recipe for NyQuil, with Absolut® vodka, Jagermeister® herbal liqueur and food coloring.

Ingredients
3/4 oz Absolut® vodka
1/4 oz Jagermeister® herbal liqueur
food coloring

Instructions
Add vodka and jagermeister to a shot glass. Add a few drops of green food coloring, mix, and serve.

Serving
Shot Glass
****

Orange Lion recipe

Description
A delicious recipe for Orange Lion, with Absolut® Mandrin vodka, DeKuyper® Peachtree schnapps and orange juice.

Ingredients
1 shot Absolut® Mandrin vodka

1 shot DeKuyper® Peachtree schnapps
1 1/2 shots orange juice

Instructions
Stir ingredients with ice and strain into a cocktail glass.

Serving
Cocktail Glass
****

Orange Smasha recipe

Description
A delicious recipe for Orange Smasha, with Absolut® Mandrin vodka, Orange Curacao liqueur, triple sec and orange sherbet.

Ingredients
1 oz Absolut® Mandrin vodka
1 oz Orange Curacao liqueur
1 oz triple sec
2 scoops orange sherbet

Instructions
Combine all ingredients in a blender with crushed ice. Blend until smooth; add more ice as required. Pour into a highball glass, add a straw, and serve.

Serving
Highball Glass
****

Pajama Jackhammer recipe

Description
A delicious recipe for Pajama Jackhammer, with guava juice, Absolut® vodka, Blue Curacao liqueur and peach schnapps.

Ingredients
3 oz guava juice

1 oz Absolut® vodka
1 oz Blue Curacao liqueur
1 oz peach schnapps

Instructions
Combine ingredients with ice in a mixing glass. Strain into a highball glass with shaved ice, and serve.

Serving
Highball Glass
****

Party Boy recipe

Description
A delicious recipe for Party Boy, with pink lemonade, Bacardi® 151 rum, triple sec, Absolut® Citron vodka, sweet and sour mix, sugar and lemon.

Ingredients
1 1/2 oz pink lemonade
1 oz Bacardi® 151 rum
1/2 oz triple sec
1/2 oz Absolut® Citron vodka
1 dash sweet and sour mix
1 tsp sugar
1 slice lemon

Instructions
Rub a lemon slice on the edge of a whiskey sour glass. Dip the edge of the glass in sugar. Add pink lemonade and a dash of sour mix. Then add Bacardi, triple sec and Absolut Citron. Stir. Lick around the edge of the glass then take the shot.

Serving
Whiskey Sour Glass
****

Party Girl recipe

Description
A delicious recipe for Party Girl, with cranberry juice, Chambord® raspberry liqueur and Absolut® Kurant vodka.

Ingredients
2 parts cranberry juice
1 part Chambord® raspberry liqueur
1 part Absolut® Kurant vodka

Instructions
Mix all ingredients in a shaker. Serve over ice, and garnish with a lime wedge.

Serving
Champagne Saucer
****

Peachy Screw recipe

Description
A delicious recipe for Peachy Screw, with Absolut® vodka, peach schnapps, Malibu® coconut rum, grenadine syrup, sweet and sour mix and orange juice.

Ingredients
1 1/2 oz Absolut® vodka
1 oz peach schnapps
1 oz Malibu® coconut rum
1 oz grenadine syrup
1 - 2 oz sweet and sour mix
1 - 2 oz orange juice

Instructions
Pour the Absolut vodka, peach schnapps, Malibu rum and grenadine into a cocktail shaker half-filled with ice cubes. Add sour mix and orange juice to taste. Shake well, and strain into a collins glass filled with ice cubes. Garnish with a maraschino cherry, and serve.

Serving
Collins Glass
****

Peekaboo recipe

Description
A delicious recipe for Peekaboo, with Absolut® Kurant vodka and orange juice.

Ingredients
2 shots Absolut® Kurant vodka
1 glass orange juice

Instructions
Pour absolut kurant into a cocktail glass, and fill with orange juice.

Serving
Cocktail Glass
****

Pelvic Crusher recipe

Description
A delicious recipe for Pelvic Crusher, with DeKuyper® Sour Apple Pucker schnapps, Absolut® vodka and Zima.

Ingredients
1 1/4 oz DeKuyper® Sour Apple Pucker schnapps
1/2 oz Absolut® vodka
4 1/2 oz Zima

Instructions
Pour the apple pucker and vodka into a highball glass filled with cracked or cubed ice. Fill with zima, stir gently and serve.

Serving
Highball Glass
****

Phantom recipe

Description
A delicious recipe for Phantom, with Licor 43® liqueur, Absolut® vodka and milk.

Ingredients
3 cl Licor 43® liqueur
3 cl Absolut® vodka
milk

Instructions
Pour licor 43 into a highball glass filled with ice cubes. Add absolut vodka, fill with milk, and mix.

Serving
Highball Glass
****

Photon Torpedo recipe

Description
A delicious recipe for Photon Torpedo, with Aftershock® Hot & Cool cinnamon schnapps and Absolut® vodka.

Ingredients
1/2 oz Aftershock® Hot & Cool cinnamon schnapps
1/2 oz Absolut® vodka

Instructions
Mix the aftershock with vodka in a shot glass.

Serving
Shot Glass
****

Phreaker Cocktail recipe

Description
A delicious recipe for Phreaker Cocktail, with Absolut® vodka, triple sec, pineapple juice, lemon juice, water, sugar and egg.

Ingredients
Absolut® vodka
1 pint triple sec
2 pints pineapple juice
1 pint lemon juice
water
1 1/2 cups sugar
1 egg white

Instructions
Fill a fifth of a bottle with equal parts of vodka and water. Add the egg white. Shake well until egg is thoroughly mixed, and pour into a punch bowl with the triple sec, juice, and sugar.

Serving
Punch Bowl
****

Pimp Cocktail recipe

Description
A delicious recipe for Pimp Cocktail, with Absolut® vodka, Blue Curacao liqueur, peach schnapps and Sunny Delight® orange juice.

Ingredients
2 oz Absolut® vodka
1 oz Blue Curacao liqueur
1 oz peach schnapps
5 oz Sunny Delight® orange juice

Instructions
Pour ingredients into a highball glass, stir, and serve.

Serving
Highball Glass
****

Pimp Punch recipe

Description
A delicious recipe for Pimp Punch, with raspberry schnapps, Absolut® Kurant vodka and Sprite® soda.

Ingredients
1 oz raspberry schnapps
1 oz Absolut® Kurant vodka
6 oz Sprite® soda

Instructions
Mix and pour over ice.

Serving
Collins Glass
****

Pine Needle recipe

Description
A delicious recipe for Pine Needle, with Absolut® vodka, triple sec, sweet and sour mix, pineapple juice and 7-Up® soda.

Ingredients
1 oz Absolut® vodka
1/2 oz triple sec
1 1/2 oz sweet and sour mix
2 oz pineapple juice
1 splash 7-Up® soda

Instructions
Pour ingredients, in the order listed, into an ice-filled highball glass. Vary to taste.

Serving
Highball Glass
****

Pineapple Snap recipe

Description
A delicious recipe for Pineapple Snap, with Ketel One® vodka, triple

sec, Absolut® Mandrin vodka and pineapple juice.

Ingredients
1 oz Ketel One® vodka
1 oz triple sec
1 oz Absolut® Mandrin vodka
5 oz pineapple juice

Instructions
Pour Ketel One vodka, triple sec and Absolut Mandrin into a cocktail shaker with ice. Shake and pour into a highball glass. Add pineapple juice, and serve.

Serving
Highball Glass
****

Pink Clyt recipe

Description
A delicious recipe for Pink Clyt, with Bacardi® white rum, Absolut® vodka, Tanqueray® gin, triple sec, cranberry juice and pineapple juice.

Ingredients
1/2 oz Bacardi® white rum
1/2 oz Absolut® vodka
1/2 oz Tanqueray® gin
1/4 oz triple sec
1 splash cranberry juice
1 splash pineapple juice

Instructions
Shake in a cocktail shaker with ice cubes. Pour into an old-fashioned glass, garnish with a cherry, and serve.

Serving
Old-Fashioned Glass
****

Pink Lemonade recipe

Description
A delicious recipe for Pink Lemonade, with Absolut® Citron vodka, Chambord® raspberry liqueur and sweet and sour mix.

Ingredients
1 1/2 oz Absolut® Citron vodka
1/2 oz Chambord® raspberry liqueur
2 oz sweet and sour mix

Instructions
Shake and serve on the rocks.

Serving
Champagne Saucer
****

Pink Millenium recipe

Description
A delicious recipe for Pink Millenium, with Absolut® Citron vodka, cranberry juice, sugar syrup and Champagne.

Ingredients
2 cl Absolut® Citron vodka
2 cl cranberry juice
1 cl sugar syrup
Champagne

Instructions
Mix vodka, cranberry juice and sugar syrup, and pour into a champagne coupe or flute. Fill with champagne or a dry sparkling wine.

Serving
Champagne Flute
****

Pink Panther #2 recipe

Description
A delicious recipe for Pink Panther #2, with Absolut® vodka, pineapple juice and cranberry juice.

Ingredients
1/3 oz Absolut® vodka
1/3 oz pineapple juice
1/3 oz cranberry juice

Instructions
Pour ingredients into a cocktail shaker with ice, and shake. Strain into a shot glass, and serve.

Serving
Shot Glass
****

Pink Penocha recipe

Description
A delicious recipe for Pink Penocha, with Everclear® alcohol, Absolut® vodka, peach schnapps, orange juice and cranberry juice.

Ingredients
3/4 liter Everclear® alcohol
1 3/4 liters Absolut® vodka
1 3/4 liters peach schnapps
1 gal orange juice
1 gal cranberry juice

Instructions
Mix all ingredients in a punch bowl. Keep chilled, and stir frequently.

Serving
Punch Bowl
****

Pink Pitch recipe

Description
A delicious recipe for Pink Pitch, with Absolut® vodka, Licor 43® liqueur, milk and grenadine syrup.

Ingredients

2 cl Absolut® vodka
4 cl Licor 43® liqueur
6 cl milk
1/2 cl grenadine syrup

Instructions
Mix in a blender on low speed and serve in a chilled glass. Garnish with a cherry.

Serving
Cocktail Glass
****

Pocima recipe

Description
A delicious recipe for Pocima, with beer, Absolut® vodka and orange juice.

Ingredients
6 cans beer
1 liter Absolut® vodka
2 gal orange juice

Instructions
Pour beer into a punch bowl. Add vodka, orange juice and plenty of ice cubes. Stir, and serve cold.

Serving
Punch Bowl
****

Poison Apple recipe

Description
A delicious recipe for Poison Apple, with apfelkorn liqueur and Absolut® vodka.

Ingredients

1 oz apfelkorn liqueur
1 oz Absolut® vodka

Instructions
Pour ingredients over ice in a shaker. Shake and strain into a shot glass.

Serving
Shot Glass
****

Porch Climber recipe

Description
A delicious recipe for Porch Climber, with Molson® Canadian beer, pink lemonade, Absolut® vodka and Canadian Club® whisky.

Ingredients
1 case Molson® Canadian beer
2 cans frozen pink lemonade
26 oz Absolut® vodka
26 oz Canadian Club® whisky

Instructions
Pour over ice in a large cooler.
****

Postman recipe

Description
A delicious recipe for Postman, with Absolut® vodka, Bacardi® 151 rum, orange juice, cranberry juice and grenadine syrup.

Ingredients
2 oz Absolut® vodka
1 oz Bacardi® 151 rum
2 oz orange juice
1 oz cranberry juice
1 splash grenadine syrup

Instructions
Chill, shake, and pour over ice cubes in a shot glass.

Serving
Shot Glass
****

Pure Pleasure recipe

Description
A delicious recipe for Pure Pleasure, with Absolut® Kurant vodka, Malibu® coconut rum, lemon juice and cranberry juice.

Ingredients
2 cl Absolut® Kurant vodka
2 cl Malibu® coconut rum
1 cl lemon juice
cranberry juice

Instructions
Shake ingredients with lots of ice cubes. Stir into a hurricane glass, and serve.

Serving
Hurricane Glass
****

Purple Fantasy recipe

Description
A delicious recipe for Purple Fantasy, with Absolut® vodka, rum, grape soda and 7-Up® soda.

Ingredients
1/2 oz Absolut® vodka
1/2 oz rum
grape soda
7-Up® soda

Instructions
Pour vodka and rum over ice in a highball glass. Top with grape soda and a splash of 7-up.

Serving
Highball Glass
****

Purple Love recipe

Description
A delicious recipe for Purple Love, with Blue Curacao liqueur, whipped cream, Chambord® raspberry liqueur, white rum, Absolut® vodka, triple sec, Sprite® soda and grenadine syrup.

Ingredients
1 oz Blue Curacao liqueur
1 oz whipped cream
1/2 oz Chambord® raspberry liqueur
1/2 oz white rum
1/2 oz Absolut® vodka
1/2 oz triple sec
2 oz Sprite® soda
2 dashes grenadine syrup

Instructions
Combine ingredients with ice in a cocktail shaker. Shake well, for about 25 seconds, and strain into a highball glass. Garnish with chocolate flakes.

Serving
Highball Glass
****

Purple Mexican recipe

Description
A delicious recipe for Purple Mexican, with Absolut® vodka, Jose Cuervo® Especial gold tequila and Grand Marnier® orange liqueur.

Ingredients

1 oz Absolut® vodka
1 oz Jose Cuervo® Especial gold tequila
1 oz Grand Marnier® orange liqueur

Instructions
Pour ingredients into a mixing glass with ice. Shake and strain into highball glass. Shoot.

Serving
Highball Glass
****

Purple People Eater recipe

Description
A delicious recipe for Purple People Eater, with Chambord® raspberry liqueur, blackberry brandy, cherry brandy, amaretto almond liqueur, Absolut® Citron vodka, orange juice, pineapple juice and grapefruit juice. Also lists similar drink re

Ingredients
2 oz Chambord® raspberry liqueur
1 oz blackberry brandy
1 oz cherry brandy
1 oz amaretto almond liqueur
1 oz Absolut® Citron vodka
1 splash orange juice
1 splash pineapple juice
1 splash grapefruit juice

Instructions
Pour ingredients over ice and shake vigorously.

Serving
Mason Jar
****

Purple Stealth recipe

Description
A delicious recipe for Purple Stealth, with Absolut® Kurant vodka and grape soda.

Ingredients
1 part Absolut® Kurant vodka
2 parts grape soda

Instructions
Pour absolut kurant into a large soft drink tumbler. Add grape soda.

Serving
Old-Fashioned Glass
****

Ragnar #3 recipe

Description
A delicious recipe for Ragnar #3, with Absolut® Kurant vodka and Sprite® soda.

Ingredients
4 cl Absolut® Kurant vodka
8 cl Sprite® soda

Instructions
Pour the vodka into a highball glass. Fill with ice cubes, and add sprite.

Serving
Highball Glass
****

Ragnar recipe

Description
A delicious recipe for Ragnar, with Absolut® Kurant vodka, limes and 7-Up® soda.

Ingredients

1 oz Absolut® Kurant vodka
limes
7-Up® soda

Instructions
Pour absolut kurant into a tall, highball glass. Add a few drops of lime juice, and fill with 7-up.

Serving
Highball Glass
****

Red Eisentrout recipe

Description
A delicious recipe for Red Eisentrout, with Absolut® vodka, Bombay Sapphire® gin, Bacardi® white rum, Grand Marnier® orange liqueur, Surge® citrus soda and cherry juice.

Ingredients
1/2 oz Absolut® vodka
1/2 oz Bombay Sapphire® gin
1/2 oz Bacardi® white rum
1/2 oz Grand Marnier® orange liqueur
Surge® citrus soda
cherry juice

Instructions
Pour liquors over ice in a collins glass, and almost fill with surge soda. Top off with cherry juice, and shake. Garnish with a cherry, and serve.

Serving
Collins Glass
****

Red Manhattan recipe

Description
A delicious recipe for Red Manhattan, with Absolut® Kurant vodka, St. Raphael® Aperitif de France wine and Angostura® bitters.

Ingredients
2 1/2 oz Absolut® Kurant vodka
3/4 oz St. Raphael® Aperitif de France wine
2 dashes Angostura® bitters

Instructions
Stir with ice to chill and strain into a chilled cocktail glass. Garnish with a cherry, and serve.

Serving
Cocktail Glass
****

Red Rock recipe

Description
A delicious recipe for Red Rock, with Absolut® vodka, wildberry schnapps and Dr. Pepper® soda.

Ingredients
1 1/2 shots Absolut® vodka
3/4 shot wildberry schnapps
1 can Dr. Pepper® soda

Instructions
Mix vodka and schnapps in the bottom of a glass. Add ice, and pour in the can of dr. pepper.

Serving
Collins Glass
****

Reggae Ambassador recipe

Description
A delicious recipe for Reggae Ambassador, with Absolut® Citron vodka, fruit juice, sugar and strawberries.

Ingredients
1 part Absolut® Citron vodka
2 parts fruit juice

4 tsp sugar
strawberries

Instructions
Fill one-quarter of a blender (half-filled with ice) with vodka. Almost fill completely with pine-orange-banana fruit juice. Add fresh strawberries and sugar, blend, and pour into glasses. Serve with an orange slice.
****

Richie 50 recipe

Description
A delicious recipe for Richie 50, with Absolut® vodka, orange juice and cherry.

Ingredients
8 oz Absolut® vodka
8 oz orange juice
1 cherry

Instructions
Pour orange juice into a 16-ounce glass half-filled with vodka. Stir, add a cherry, and serve.

Serving
Hurricane Glass
****

Rising Skirt recipe

Description
A delicious recipe for Rising Skirt, with Absolut® Mandrin vodka, Smirnoff® vodka, Cointreau® orange liqueur, Midori® melon liqueur, banana liqueur, raspberry liqueur, sweet and sour mix and pineapple juice. Also lists simi

Ingredients
1/2 oz Absolut® Mandrin vodka
1/2 oz Smirnoff® vodka
1/4 oz Cointreau® orange liqueur
1/4 oz Midori® melon liqueur

1/2 oz banana liqueur
1/4 oz raspberry liqueur
1 splash sweet and sour mix
1 splash pineapple juice

Instructions
Add all ingredients to a shaker and shake well. Pour into a whiskey sour glass with ice and top with an orange slice.

Serving
Whiskey Sour Glass
****

Roffsing recipe

Description
A delicious recipe for Roffsing, with Passoa® liqueur, Absolut® vodka, lime juice, pear soda and whipped cream.

Ingredients
4 cl Passoa® liqueur
4 cl Absolut® vodka
2 splashes lime juice
pear soda
1 1/2 oz whipped cream

Instructions
Pour passoa, vodka, lime juice and pear soda into a collins glass half-filled with ice cubes. Stir, top with cream, and serve.

Serving
Collins Glass
****

Rumka recipe

Description
A delicious recipe for Rumka, with Absolut® vodka and Captain Morgan® Original spiced rum.

Ingredients

1 oz Absolut® vodka
1 oz Captain Morgan® Original spiced rum

Instructions
Mix equal parts of vodka and rum, pour over ice in a shot glass, and serve.

Serving
Shot Glass
****

Russian Sarin recipe

Description
A delicious recipe for Russian Sarin, with Absolut® Kurant vodka, Midori® melon liqueur and Schweppes® Russian tonic water.

Ingredients
2 cl Absolut® Kurant vodka
2 cl Midori® melon liqueur
Schweppes® Russian tonic water

Instructions
Pour vodka and liqueur into a highball glass over one or two ice cubes. Fill with schweppes russian, and serve.

Serving
Highball Glass
****

Sabra recipe

Description
A delicious recipe for Sabra, with Absolut® Mandrin vodka and Godiva® chocolate liqueur.

Ingredients
3/4 oz Absolut® Mandrin vodka
3/4 oz Godiva® chocolate liqueur

Instructions

Chill together in the shaker and strain into a shot glass.

Serving
Shot Glass
****

Salt and Pepper Martini recipe

Description
A delicious recipe for Salt and Pepper Martini, with vermouth and Absolut® Peppar vodka.

Ingredients
1/8 oz vermouth
2 oz Absolut® Peppar vodka

Instructions
Combine vermouth and absolut peppar in a mixing glass over ice. Stir, strain into a salt-rimmed cocktail glass, and serve.

Serving
Cocktail Glass
****

San Diego Silver Bullet recipe

Description
A delicious recipe for San Diego Silver Bullet, with Absolut® vodka and sambuca.

Ingredients
2 oz Absolut® vodka
2 oz sambuca

Instructions
Shake the ingredients over ice, strain into an old-fashioned glass and serve. Down it in one.

Serving
Old-Fashioned Glass
****

Scarlet Fever recipe

Description
A delicious recipe for Scarlet Fever, with Absolut® vodka, white rum, London dry gin and cranberry juice.

Ingredients
12 - 14 oz Absolut® vodka
12 - 14 oz white rum
6 - 8 oz London dry gin
6 oz cranberry juice

Instructions
Mix together and shake, pour into a draft glass. Add 3 ice cubes and garnish with a lemon wheel on the side.

Serving
Beer Mug
****

Schnapp It Up recipe

Description
A delicious recipe for Schnapp It Up, with peach schnapps, wildberry schnapps, Absolut® vodka and cranberry juice.

Ingredients
1 part peach schnapps
1 part wildberry schnapps
1 part Absolut® vodka
3 parts cranberry juice

Instructions
Stir all ingredients together in a mixing glass. Strain over ice in a cocktail glass, and serve.

Serving
Cocktail Glass
****

Scotty Boy recipe

Description
A delicious recipe for Scotty Boy, with Absolut® Kurant vodka, sweet and sour mix and soda water.

Ingredients
Absolut® Kurant vodka
fill with sweet and sour mix
1 splash soda water

Instructions
Pour a lot of kurant into ice filled glass. Fill with sour mix. Shake, always shake and add a splash of soda.

Serving
Highball Glass
****

Screwed Driver recipe

Description
A delicious recipe for Screwed Driver, with Absolut® Mandrin vodka, lemonade, cranberry juice and ice.

Ingredients
1 1/2 oz Absolut® Mandrin vodka
fill with lemonade
1 dash cranberry juice
ice

Instructions
Fill glass with ice. Add vodka. Fill with lemonade and add a dash of cranberry juice.

Serving
Old-Fashioned Glass
****

Scrumdriver recipe

Description
A delicious recipe for Scrumdriver, with Tropicana® orange juice,

Absolut® vodka and lime juice.

Ingredients
4 1/2 oz Tropicana® orange juice
1 1/2 oz Absolut® vodka
4 dashes lime juice

Instructions
Mix the vodka and orange juice in a chilled highball glass over ice. Add several dashes of lime juice at your discretion.

Serving
Highball Glass
****

Seizure recipe

Description
A delicious recipe for Seizure, with Absolut® vodka, peach schnapps, orange juice, cranberry juice and apple juice.

Ingredients
4 shots Absolut® vodka
3 shots peach schnapps
3 oz orange juice
3 oz cranberry juice
3 oz apple juice

Instructions
Pour ingredients over crushed ice in a hurricane glass. Mix through a couple times and serve.

Serving
Hurricane Glass
****

Serena recipe

Description
A delicious recipe for Serena, with Absolut® vodka, strawberry vodka, dry vermouth, pineapple juice, Blue Curacao liqueur and lemon juice.

Ingredients
2/5 cl Absolut® vodka
1/5 cl strawberry vodka
1/5 cl dry vermouth
1/10 cl pineapple juice
1/10 cl Blue Curacao liqueur
5 drops lemon juice

Instructions
First of all put in the mixing glass absolut vodka then strawberry vodka, dry vermouth, pineapple juice, blue curacao and lemon juice. Now shake with ice and fill up the glass.

Serving
Cocktail Glass
****

Sex On An Arizona Beach recipe

Description
A delicious recipe for Sex On An Arizona Beach, with Absolut® vodka, peach schnapps, grapefruit juice, lime juice and grenadine syrup.

Ingredients
2 shots Absolut® vodka
2 shots peach schnapps
1 dash grapefruit juice
1 dash lime juice
1 splash grenadine syrup

Instructions
Mix ingredients and add some ice.

Serving
Hurricane Glass
****

Sex on the Beach #4 recipe

Description
A delicious recipe for Sex on the Beach #4, with Absolut® vodka, Midori® melon liqueur, Chambord® raspberry liqueur, grapefruit juice and cranberry juice.

Ingredients
1/3 oz Absolut® vodka
1/3 oz Midori® melon liqueur
1/3 oz Chambord® raspberry liqueur
1 splash grapefruit juice
3 squirts cranberry juice

Instructions
This can be on the rocks or up... but best on the rocks! Start with the Midori since it is heaviest, then the Chambord and the Absolut. Fill the glass 2/3 full with Cranberry juice, and then a splash of grapefruit for color. It should be an orangish-red color. Garnish with several cherries.

Serving
Cocktail Glass
****

Sex On The Beach #6 recipe

Description
A delicious recipe for Sex On The Beach #6, with Absolut® Citron vodka, strawberry schnapps, orange juice and cream.

Ingredients
1 1/4 oz Absolut® Citron vodka
1 oz strawberry schnapps
5 - 6 oz orange juice
1/4 oz cream

Instructions
Highball glass 1/2 full ice. Add vodka and schnapps. Fill to near top with OJ, amount depends on ice and glass size. Add cream last and stir. May be served up after mixing. The amount of OJ and dairy cream may be adjusted to taste.

Serving

Highball Glass
****

Sex on the Brain recipe

Description
A delicious recipe for Sex on the Brain, with Arrow® peach schnapps, Absolut® vodka, Midori® melon liqueur, pineapple juice, orange juice and sloe gin.

Ingredients
1 oz Arrow® peach schnapps
1 oz Absolut® vodka
1 oz Midori® melon liqueur
pineapple juice
orange juice
1 tbsp sloe gin

Instructions
Fill glass with ice, insert a straw and then add the first three ingredients (Vodka, Midori, Schnapps) then layer the juices using a barspoon to get a separation of alcohol and mixers. Leave a little room at top of glass to float the Sloe gin on top.

Garnish with a cherry and orange wedge.

*The drink should look like a Stop Light. Green at the bottom, yellow in the middle and red on top.

Serving
Hurricane Glass
****

Sexual Trance recipe

Description
A delicious recipe for Sexual Trance, with Absolut® Citron vodka, Midori® melon liqueur, Chambord® raspberry liqueur, orange juice, pineapple juice and sweet and sour mix.

Ingredients

1 oz Absolut® Citron vodka
1/2 oz Midori® melon liqueur
1/2 oz Chambord® raspberry liqueur
1/2 oz orange juice
1/2 oz pineapple juice
1 splash sweet and sour mix

Instructions
Shake well with ice and strain over ice cherry garnish.

Serving
Collins Glass
****

Shark Attack recipe

Description
A delicious recipe for Shark Attack, with lemonade, water and Absolut® vodka.

Ingredients
1 can lemonade concentrate
3 cans water
1 1/2 cups Absolut® vodka

Instructions
Mix lemonade and water according to instructions on back of can. If the instructions say to add 4 1/3 cans of water do so. Mix into pitcher. Add 1 1/2 cup of Vodka (Absolut). Mix well. Pour into glass of crushed ice. Excellent!

Serving
Pitcher
****

Shetty Classic recipe

Description
A delicious recipe for Shetty Classic, with Ricard® pastis, Bacardi® white rum and Absolut® vodka.

Ingredients
1 oz Ricard® pastis
1 oz Bacardi® white rum
1 oz Absolut® vodka

Instructions
Pour Ricard, Bacardi rum and Absolut vodka into a bowl filled with sugar. Set on fire (use extreme caution) and let the sugar dissolve. Allow the drink to cool, and serve in a cocktail glass.

Serving
Cocktail Glass
****

Skittle recipe

Description
A delicious recipe for Skittle, with Absolut® vodka, banana liqueur, Kool-Aid® Watermelon-Cherry and crushed ice.

Ingredients
1 1/2 oz Absolut® vodka
1 1/2 oz banana liqueur
Kool-Aid® Watermelon-Cherry
crushed ice

Instructions
Add Absolut Vodka and Banana Liqueur to Collins glass. Fill glass 3/4 full with Kool-Aid. Add crushed ice, stir, and serve.

Kool-Aid flavor determines what flavor Skittle you get.

Serving
Collins Glass
****

Skylab Fallout recipe

Description
A delicious recipe for Skylab Fallout, with Absolut® vodka, Bacardi® 151 rum, gold tequila, gin, Everclear® alcohol, Blue Curacao liqueur and

pineapple juice.

Ingredients
1/2 oz Absolut® vodka
1/2 oz Bacardi® 151 rum
1/2 oz gold tequila
1/2 oz gin
1/2 oz Everclear® alcohol
1/2 oz Blue Curacao liqueur
1/2 oz pineapple juice

Instructions
Put plenty of ice in glass pour rum and everclear first refill with ice - put your tequila, gin, vodka and your blue curacao in. Put your pinapple juice in and shake serve with a lemon slice and cherry.

Serving
Hurricane Glass
****

Slemmig Slyna recipe

Description
A delicious recipe for Slemmig Slyna, with Absolut® vodka, Midori® melon liqueur, kiwi liqueur and sweet and sour mix.

Ingredients
3 cl Absolut® vodka
2 cl Midori® melon liqueur
2 cl kiwi liqueur
sweet and sour mix

Instructions
Mix vodka and midori and kiwi with ice. Add sourmix. Shake. Fill with soda. Decorate glass with pineapple.

Serving
Highball Glass
****

Slippery Box recipe

Description
A delicious recipe for Slippery Box, with Absolut® Citron vodka, Southern Comfort® peach liqueur, Everclear® alcohol and Kool-Aid® Grape mix.

Ingredients
1 1/2 oz Absolut® Citron vodka
1 1/2 oz Southern Comfort® peach liqueur
1 1/2 oz Everclear® alcohol
fill with Kool-Aid® Grape mix

Instructions
In a glass, put in all liquor and then fill the remaining glass with the kool-aid.

Serving
Old-Fashioned Glass
****

Smoked Martini recipe

Description
A delicious recipe for Smoked Martini, with Glenlivet® Scotch whisky, Absolut® vodka and lemon.

Ingredients
1 part Glenlivet® Scotch whisky
1 part Absolut® vodka
1 lemon slice

Instructions
Pour the scotch and vodka into a pitcher, and squeeze in the juice from a slice of lemon. Mix with ice, let stand for a few minutes to chill, then pour into glasses with ice. Add lemon to taste.

Serving
Cocktail Glass
****

Smurf Piss #2 recipe

Description
A delicious recipe for Smurf Piss #2, with Absolut® vodka, DeKuyper Island Blue Pucker and lemonade.

Ingredients
1 oz Absolut® vodka
1 oz DeKuyper Island Blue Pucker
5 oz lemonade

Instructions
Pour vodka and schnapps over ice in a highball glass. Add lemonade, and serve.

Serving
Highball Glass
****

Snowshot recipe

Description
A delicious recipe for Snowshot, with Absolut® Citron vodka, lemon sherbet, lemons and sugar.

Ingredients
3 oz Absolut® Citron vodka
1 scoop lemon sherbet
juice of 1/2 lemons
1 sugar cube

Instructions
Throw all ingredients into blender. Add sugar to taste, sweet lemons dont need more than one cube. Blend until the consistancy resembles a daiquiri.

Serving
Highball Glass
****

South Beach Martini recipe

Description
A delicious recipe for South Beach Martini, with orange vodka, Absolut® Citron vodka, Cointreau® orange liqueur, lime juice and orange.

Ingredients
2 oz orange vodka
2 oz Absolut® Citron vodka
3/4 oz Cointreau® orange liqueur
3/4 oz lime juice
1 twist orange peel

Instructions
Shake well with ice. Strain into large martini glass. Garnish with twist of orange peel.

Serving
Cocktail Glass
****

Southern Blast recipe

Description
A delicious recipe for Southern Blast, with Absolut® vodka, Absolut® Kurant vodka, Goldschlager® cinnamon schnapps, Southern Comfort® peach liqueur and fruit juice.

Ingredients
1 oz Absolut® vodka
3/4 oz Absolut® Kurant vodka
1/2 oz Goldschlager® cinnamon schnapps
1 oz Southern Comfort® peach liqueur
fill with fruit juice

Instructions
Just pour it all in a glass. Stir it if you really feel the need to. I usually just pour in the alcohol and let the fruit juice do the mixing for me. For the best results, try and use that Minute Maid Fruit Punch. That stuff works very well. I advise against using any sort of "all-citrus" fruit juice, even OJ.

Serving
Beer Pilsner
****

Southern Peach recipe

Description
A delicious recipe for Southern Peach, with Southern Comfort® peach liqueur, peach schnapps, triple sec and Absolut® Citron vodka.

Ingredients
2 oz Southern Comfort® peach liqueur
1 1/2 oz peach schnapps
1/2 oz triple sec
1 oz Absolut® Citron vodka

Instructions
Add all with ice shack and strain.

Serving
Old-Fashioned Glass
****

Spice and Ice recipe

Description
A delicious recipe for Spice and Ice, with Absolut® Citron vodka, Goldschlager® cinnamon schnapps and Dr. Pepper® soda.

Ingredients
1 part Absolut® Citron vodka
1 part Goldschlager® cinnamon schnapps
2 parts Dr. Pepper® soda

Instructions
Mix all three on the rocks.

Serving
Highball Glass
****

Spooky Juice recipe

Description
A delicious recipe for Spooky Juice, with Absolut® vodka, Blue Curacao liqueur, grenadine syrup and orange juice.

Ingredients
1 oz Absolut® vodka
2 dashes Blue Curacao liqueur
1 dash grenadine syrup
fill with orange juice

Instructions
Stir together with ice.

Serving
Highball Glass
****

Sprawling Dubinsky recipe

Description
A delicious recipe for Sprawling Dubinsky, with Johnnie Walker® Red Label Scotch whisky, Johnnie Walker® Black Label Scotch whisky, Absolut® Citron vodka and amaretto almond liqueur.

Ingredients
1 part Johnnie Walker® Red Label Scotch whisky
1 part Johnnie Walker® Black Label Scotch whisky
1 part Absolut® Citron vodka
1 dash amaretto almond liqueur

Instructions
First, add one part of Johnnie Walker Red. Next add one part Johnnie Walker Black, followed by another part of Absolut Citron. Finally, throw in a touch of amaretto, for flavor.

Serving
Shot Glass
****

Springtime recipe

Description
A delicious recipe for Springtime, with Absolut® Kurant vodka, lime juice, cranberry juice and bitter lemon soda.

Ingredients
4 cl Absolut® Kurant vodka
1 cl lime juice
10 cl cranberry juice
3 cl bitter lemon soda

Instructions
Poor ingredients over lots of ice.Garnish with slice of lime.

Serving
Highball Glass
****

Stardust recipe

Description
A delicious recipe for Stardust, with Absolut® Citron vodka, DeKuyper® Peachtree schnapps, Blue Curacao liqueur, sweet and sour mix, pineapple juice and grenadine syrup.

Ingredients
1/2 oz Absolut® Citron vodka
1/2 oz DeKuyper® Peachtree schnapps
1/2 oz Blue Curacao liqueur
1 oz sweet and sour mix
1 oz pineapple juice
1 splash grenadine syrup

Instructions
Fill shaker cup with ice. Pour in all ingredients. Shake and strain into shooter glass of preference.

Serving

Cordial Glass
****

Start Me Up recipe

Description
A delicious recipe for Start Me Up, with Absolut® vodka, tequila, Absolut® Kurant vodka and Bacardi® dark rum.

Ingredients
3 cl Absolut® vodka
1 cl tequila
1 cl Absolut® Kurant vodka
1 cl Bacardi® dark rum

Instructions
Mix everything in a container (bottle, glass etc.), then it is ready for consumption.

Serving
Shot Glass
****

Strap-O-Nilla Juice recipe

Description
A delicious recipe for Strap-O-Nilla Juice, with Absolut® Vanilia vodka, orange juice, pineapple juice and strawberry daiquiri mix.

Ingredients
3 oz Absolut® Vanilia vodka
2 oz orange juice
2 oz pineapple juice
2 oz strawberry daiquiri mix

Instructions
Pour all ingredients into a mixing glass, and shake well. Pour into a highball glass filled with ice, and serve.

Serving

Highball Glass
****

Sunflower Highball recipe

Description
A delicious recipe for Sunflower Highball, with Absolut® vodka, Licor 43® liqueur and orange juice.

Ingredients
1 oz Absolut® vodka
1 oz Licor 43® liqueur
5 oz fresh orange juice

Instructions
Build over ice in a highball glass. Dust with nutmeg, and serve.

Serving
Highball Glass
****

Sunset Breeze recipe

Description
A delicious recipe for Sunset Breeze, with Absolut® vodka, Absolut® Citron vodka, Bacardi® Tropico rum, lime juice, cherry heering and simple syrup.

Ingredients
1/2 oz Absolut® vodka
1/2 oz Absolut® Citron vodka
1 1/2 oz Bacardi® Tropico rum
1/2 oz fresh lime juice
1/2 oz cherry heering
1/2 oz simple syrup

Instructions
Shake all ingredients with ice and strain into a cocktail glass. Garnish with a twist of orange peel, and serve.

Serving

Cocktail Glass
****

Suntory Cocktail recipe

Description
A delicious recipe for Suntory Cocktail, with Absolut® Citron vodka, Midori® melon liqueur and grapefruit juice.

Ingredients
1 1/2 oz Absolut® Citron vodka
1 oz Midori® melon liqueur
1 oz fresh grapefruit juice

Instructions
Shake, strain into an iced cocktail glass, and serve.

Serving
Cocktail Glass
****

Swedish Blue recipe

Description
A delicious recipe for Swedish Blue, with Absolut® vodka, armagnac, blueberry syrup, Blue Curacao liqueur and lime juice.

Ingredients
1 1/2 oz Absolut® vodka
1/2 oz armagnac
1/2 oz blueberry syrup
1 tsp Blue Curacao liqueur
1/3 oz lime juice

Instructions
Shake with a glassful of broken ice and pour unstrained into an old-fashioned glass. Garnish with a slice of orange and a blue cherry, and serve.

Serving

Old-Fashioned Glass
****

Swedish Polar Bear recipe

Description
A delicious recipe for Swedish Polar Bear, with Absolut® vodka, Blue Curacao liqueur and Sprite® soda.

Ingredients
4 cl Absolut® vodka
2 cl Blue Curacao liqueur
Sprite® soda

Instructions
Combine and mix absolut vodka and blue curacao over ice cubes in a collins glass. Fill with sprite, and serve.

Serving
Collins Glass
****

Swedish Polar Bear recipe

Description
A delicious recipe for Swedish Polar Bear, with Absolut® vodka, Blue Curacao liqueur and Sprite® soda.

Ingredients
4 cl Absolut® vodka
2 cl Blue Curacao liqueur
Sprite® soda

Instructions
Mix absolut vodka and blue curacao in a glass with ice cubes. Fill with sprite, and serve.

Serving
Cocktail Glass
****

Tanga recipe

Description
A delicious recipe for Tanga, with Tang® powdered soft drink, Absolut® vodka and ice.

Ingredients
2 parts Tang® powdered soft drink
1 part Absolut® vodka
5 handfuls ice

Instructions
In blender add Orange Tang Mix, Absolut Vodka, and ice. Blend until smooth.

Serving
Hurricane Glass
****

Taste of Winter recipe

Description
A delicious recipe for Taste of Winter, with Absolut® Citron vodka, cherry heering, Galliano® herbal liqueur and Schweppes® Russian tonic water.

Ingredients
4 cl Absolut® Citron vodka
1 cl cherry heering
1 cl Galliano® herbal liqueur
fill with Schweppes® Russian tonic water

Instructions
Build in in the glass. Plenty of ice cubes

Serving
Highball Glass
****

Tattooed Love Goddess recipe

Description
A delicious recipe for Tattooed Love Goddess, with Absolut® vodka, vanilla schnapps, Godiva® chocolate liqueur and half-and-half.

Ingredients
1 oz Absolut® vodka
1 oz vanilla schnapps
1 1/2 oz Godiva® chocolate liqueur
fill with half-and-half

Instructions
Fill glass w/ ice, add all liquers, top off w/cream and shake well.

Serving
Cocktail Glass
****

Texas Pink Cloud recipe

Description
A delicious recipe for Texas Pink Cloud, with Bacardi® white rum, Absolut® vodka, Jose Cuervo® Especial gold tequila, grenadine syrup, pina colada mix, sweet and sour mix, margarita mix and ice.

Ingredients
3 oz Bacardi® white rum
2 oz Absolut® vodka
1 oz Jose Cuervo® Especial gold tequila
1/2 oz grenadine syrup
3 oz pina colada mix
2 oz sweet and sour mix
1 oz margarita mix
3 - 4 cups ice

Instructions
Pour all ingredients into a blender, add 3 - 4 cups of ice and blend until all ice is chopped fine. Should be the consistentency of a daiquiri or colada. Pour into a pitcher ready to serve.

Serving

Pitcher
****

The Abba recipe

Description
A delicious recipe for The Abba, with Absolut® Citron vodka, Sprite® soda, lime and ice cubes.

Ingredients
4 oz Absolut® Citron vodka
2 1/2 oz Sprite® soda
1 twist lime peel
ice cubes

Instructions
Mix absolut citron with sprite, add a twist of lime, and stir.

Serving
Cocktail Glass
****

The Betty Ford recipe

Description
A delicious recipe for The Betty Ford, with Absolut® Citron vodka, Sprite® soda and grenadine syrup.

Ingredients
1 1/2 oz Absolut® Citron vodka
10 oz Sprite® soda
1/2 oz grenadine syrup

Instructions
Add grenadine (based on desired sweetness), followed by absolut. Add ice and then sprite (her preferred mixing).

Serving
Collins Glass
****

The Bozek recipe

Description
A delicious recipe for The Bozek, with Absolut® vodka, lime juice, pineapple juice and ice cubes.

Ingredients
3 oz Absolut® vodka
1/4 cup lime juice
1/2 cup pineapple juice
ice cubes

Instructions
Add ingrediants in following order: ice, vodka, lime, and then pineapple. Stir vigorously.

Serving
Old-Fashioned Glass
****

The BV recipe

Description
A delicious recipe for The BV, with Absolut® vodka, orange juice, tomato juice and ice cubes.

Ingredients
2 oz Absolut® vodka
4 oz orange juice
1 oz tomato juice
6 - 7 ice cubes

Instructions
Add ice first, then vodka, OJ and tomato juice. Give a light stir.

Substitute Bloody Mary Mix for Tomato Juice for a spicier taste.

Serving
Mason Jar
****

The Cherry Bomb recipe

Description
A delicious recipe for The Cherry Bomb, with cherry, Absolut® vodka, cinnamon schnapps and Bacardi® light rum.

Ingredients
1 cherry
2 tsp Absolut® vodka
1 tsp cinnamon schnapps
1 tsp Bacardi® light rum

Instructions
Put the cherry into the shot glass. Add the Cinnamon Schnapps (be careful it is real strong). Then add the Rum and top of with the Vodka. More Vodka can be used. Slam it.

Serving
Shot Glass

****

The Fuzzy Magnum recipe

Description
A delicious recipe for The Fuzzy Magnum, with grenadine syrup, peach schnapps, Absolut® Mandrin vodka, triple sec, orange juice and lemon.

Ingredients
1 1/2 oz grenadine syrup
1 1/2 oz peach schnapps
1 oz Absolut® Mandrin vodka
1 oz triple sec
2 oz orange juice
1 lemon wedge

Instructions
Mix all ingredients (except lemon wedge) into shaker. Fill glass with ice and pour until about 1/4 inch remains in glass. Squeeze lemon wedge into drink then drop lemon wedge in (for color and flavor).

Serving

Highball Glass
****

The Hollywood recipe

Description
A delicious recipe for The Hollywood, with Absolut® vodka, DeKuyper® Razzmatazz liqueur and pineapple juice.

Ingredients
3/4 oz Absolut® vodka
3/4 oz DeKuyper® Razzmatazz liqueur
fill with pineapple juice

Instructions
Mix with ice and strain into an ice-filled highball glass.

Serving
Highball Glass
****

The Lowee recipe

Description
A delicious recipe for The Lowee, with Absolut® vodka, triple sec and lemonade.

Ingredients
2 1/2 oz Absolut® vodka
2 oz triple sec
fill with lemonade

Instructions
Stir it up, and serve.

Serving
Cocktail Glass
****

The Lunchbox recipe

Description
A delicious recipe for The Lunchbox, with Midori® melon liqueur, Malibu® coconut rum, Absolut® Citron vodka, peach schnapps, pineapple juice, sweet and sour mix and 7-Up® soda.

Ingredients
1/2 oz Midori® melon liqueur
1/2 oz Malibu® coconut rum
1/2 oz Absolut® Citron vodka
1/2 oz peach schnapps
1 splash pineapple juice
1 splash sweet and sour mix
1 splash 7-Up® soda

Instructions
Chill and strain into a cocktail glass.

Serving
Cocktail Glass
****

The Triple recipe

Description
A delicious recipe for The Triple, with Absolut® vodka, Jagermeister® herbal liqueur and Goldschlager® cinnamon schnapps.

Ingredients
1/3 shot Absolut® vodka
1/2 shot Jagermeister® herbal liqueur
1/2 shot Goldschlager® cinnamon schnapps

Instructions
Straight out of the freezer, pour into a double shot glass the vodka, then J?germeister, then Goldschlager.

Serving
Shot Glass
****

Thirsty Marine recipe

Description
A delicious recipe for Thirsty Marine, with Red Bull® energy drink, Absolut® vodka, triple sec, Jagermeister® herbal liqueur, peach schnapps, Southern Comfort® peach liqueur and orange juice. Also lists similar drink recipe

Ingredients
4 oz Red Bull® energy drink
1/4 oz Absolut® vodka
1/4 oz triple sec
1/2 oz Jagermeister® herbal liqueur
1/2 oz peach schnapps
1/2 oz 100 proof Southern Comfort® peach liqueur
2 oz orange juice

Instructions
Pour all ingredients over ice in a highball glass. Stir, and serve.

Serving
Highball Glass
****

Three Wise Men #3 recipe

Description
A delicious recipe for Three Wise Men #3, with Jagermeister® herbal liqueur, Absolut® vodka and Rumple Minze® peppermint liqueur.

Ingredients
2/3 oz Jagermeister® herbal liqueur
2/3 oz Absolut® vodka
2/3 oz Rumple Minze® peppermint liqueur

Instructions
Pour 2/3 of an oz. of each ingredient into a shot glass and drink.

Serving
Shot Glass
****

Thunder King recipe

Description
A delicious recipe for Thunder King, with whiskey, coffee, milk, Absolut® Citron vodka and ice cubes.

Ingredients
30 ml whiskey
10 ml coffee
5 ml milk
2 ml Absolut® Citron vodka
4 parts ice cubes

Instructions
Just mix it and shake it.

Serving
Whiskey Sour Glass
****

Thunder Peel recipe

Description
A delicious recipe for Thunder Peel, with Surge® citrus soda, Absolut® Citron vodka, strawberry daiquiri mix and peach schnapps.

Ingredients
1 part Surge® citrus soda
2 shots Absolut® Citron vodka
1 part strawberry daiquiri mix
2 parts peach schnapps

Instructions
Shake it all chill and serve.

Serving
Margarita Glass
****

Tie Me To The Bedpost - Hawaiian recipe

Description
A delicious recipe for Tie Me To The Bedpost - Hawaiian, with Absolut® Citron vodka, Captain Morgan® Parrot Bay coconut rum, Midori® melon liqueur, sweet and sour mix and 7-Up® soda.

Ingredients
1 oz Absolut® Citron vodka
1 oz Captain Morgan® Parrot Bay coconut rum
1 oz Midori® melon liqueur
1 splash sweet and sour mix
1 splash 7-Up® soda

Instructions
Shake with ice and strain into an over-sized martini glass. There should be a slight amount of foam from the 7-up.

Serving
Cocktail Glass
****

Tie Me To The Bedpost Baby recipe

Description
A delicious recipe for Tie Me To The Bedpost Baby, with Midori® melon liqueur, sloe gin, Absolut® vodka, Southern Comfort® peach liqueur, Chambord® raspberry liqueur, pineapple juice and cranberry juice. Also lists similar

Ingredients
1 part Midori® melon liqueur
1 part sloe gin
1 part Absolut® vodka
1 part Southern Comfort® peach liqueur
1 part Chambord® raspberry liqueur
1 part pineapple juice
1 part cranberry juice

Instructions
Mix with ice in a hurricane glass.

Serving

Hurricane Glass
****

Tight Snatch recipe

Description
A delicious recipe for Tight Snatch, with ice, Absolut® vodka, peach schnapps, orange juice and cranberry juice.

Ingredients
ice
1 shot Absolut® vodka
1 shot peach schnapps
orange juice
cranberry juice

Instructions
Shake with ice. Serve in ice-filled glass.

Serving
Old-Fashioned Glass
****

Tom Collins ala Olsen recipe

Description
A delicious recipe for Tom Collins ala Olsen, with Absolut® vodka, collins mix and Sprite® soda.

Ingredients
4 cl Absolut® vodka
2 cl collins mix
8 cl Light Sprite® soda

Instructions
Just mix the ingredients.

Serving
Highball Glass
****

Touchdown recipe

Description
A delicious recipe for Touchdown, with Absolut® Mandrin vodka and Red Bull® energy drink.

Ingredients
1 oz Absolut® Mandrin vodka
6 oz Red Bull® energy drink

Instructions
Fill a shot glass with Absolut Mandrin. Seperately, fill a highball glass a little less then 1/2 way with Red Bull. Drop the shot class of Absolut Mandarin into the glass of Red Bull and slam it.

Serving
Highball Glass
****

Triple Asp recipe

Description
A delicious recipe for Triple Asp, with Absolut® vodka, Absolut® Citron vodka, Absolut® Kurant vodka and Sprite® soda.

Ingredients
2 cl Absolut® vodka
2 cl Absolut® Citron vodka
2 cl Absolut® Kurant vodka
fill with Sprite® soda

Instructions
Poor the ingredients in a glass. Ice if preferred. Drink it on a hot summernight.

Serving
Highball Glass
****

Triple Threat recipe

Description
A delicious recipe for Triple Threat, with Absolut® Citron vodka, triple sec, peach schnapps, Minute Maid® orange juice and 7-Up® soda.

Ingredients
1 oz Absolut® Citron vodka
2 oz triple sec
1 oz peach schnapps
1 1/2 oz Minute Maid® orange juice
1/2 oz 7-Up® soda

Instructions
Pour Absolut Citron into a highball glass filled with ice. Add peach schnapps and triple sec. Top off with orange juice and 7-up, to taste, and serve.

Serving
Highball Glass
****

Tropical Binalada recipe

Description
A delicious recipe for Tropical Binalada, with Absolut® vodka, sweet and sour mix, creme de bananes, pineapple juice, ice and club soda.

Ingredients
1 oz Absolut® vodka
2 oz sweet and sour mix
1 oz creme de bananes
4 oz pineapple juice
ice
top with club soda

Instructions

Combine first 5 ingredients into a cocktail shaker. Shake well. Pour the contents unstrained into a collins glass and top up with club soda.

Serving
Collins Glass
****

Tropical Hooter recipe

Description
A delicious recipe for Tropical Hooter, with Chambord® raspberry liqueur, 7-Up® soda, Absolut® Citron vodka and watermelon schnapps.

Ingredients
1/2 oz Chambord® raspberry liqueur
1/3 oz 7-Up® soda
1/3 oz Absolut® Citron vodka
1/3 oz watermelon schnapps

Instructions
Mix and pour into shotglass.

Serving
Shot Glass
****

Tropical Life Saver #2 recipe

Description
A delicious recipe for Tropical Life Saver #2, with Midori® melon liqueur, Malibu® coconut rum, Absolut® Citron vodka, pineapple juice, sweet and sour mix and 7-Up® soda.

Ingredients
3/4 oz Midori® melon liqueur
3/4 oz Malibu® coconut rum
1/2 oz Absolut® Citron vodka
2 oz pineapple juice
1 oz sweet and sour mix
1 splash 7-Up® soda

Instructions
Mix together in a tall glass.

Serving
Collins Glass
****

Tropical Lust recipe

Description
A delicious recipe for Tropical Lust, with sloe gin, Absolut® vodka, Southern Comfort® peach liqueur, Midori® melon liqueur, pineapple juice and ice.

Ingredients
1 1/2 oz sloe gin
1 oz Absolut® vodka
1/2 oz Southern Comfort® peach liqueur
1/2 oz Midori® melon liqueur
fill with pineapple juice
ice

Instructions
Fill glass with ice, add gin and vodka. Almost fill with pineapple juice, then add southern comfort and melon liqueur. The drink can also be made frozen by adding 1 1/2 scoops of ice and blending.

Serving
Hurricane Glass
****

Tropical Orgasm #3 recipe

Description
A delicious recipe for Tropical Orgasm #3, with Absolut® Citron vodka, Absolut® Mandrin vodka, peach schnapps, strawberry liqueur, cranberry juice, orange juice, pineapple juice and maraschino cherry.

Ingredients
1/3 oz Absolut® Citron vodka
1/3 oz Absolut® Mandrin vodka

1/3 oz peach schnapps
1 splash strawberry liqueur
1 splash cranberry juice
1 splash orange juice
1 splash pineapple juice
1 maraschino cherry

Instructions
Mix all ingredients in shaker. Pour over ice. Garnish with cherry.

Serving
Collins Glass
****

Tropical Orgasm recipe

Description
A delicious recipe for Tropical Orgasm, with pink lemonade, Absolut® vodka, Mr & Mrs T® strawberry daiquiri mix and Captain Morgan® Original spiced rum.

Ingredients
pink lemonade
1/2 fifth Absolut® vodka
1/4 bottle Mr & Mrs T® strawberry daiquiri mix
1 splash Captain Morgan® Original spiced rum

Instructions
Start with 3/4 of a pitcher with pink lemonade. Then add the vodka. Mix till you can barely taste the vodka, then add the strawberry daiquiri mix, then a splash of rum. (Just a bit, do not add too much) Stir and then chill.
****

Tropical Storm Jack recipe

Description
A delicious recipe for Tropical Storm Jack, with Absolut® Kurant vodka, coconut rum, Chambord® raspberry liqueur, grenadine syrup and pineapple juice.

Ingredients

1/4 oz Absolut® Kurant vodka
1 oz coconut rum
1/4 oz Chambord® raspberry liqueur
1 splash grenadine syrup
fill with pineapple juice

Instructions
Put all in hi-ball glass and shake garnish w/lime.

Serving
Highball Glass
****

Troutie recipe

Description
A delicious recipe for Troutie, with Absolut® Mandrin vodka, grapefruit juice and 7-Up® soda.

Ingredients
2 oz Absolut® Mandrin vodka
1 - 2 oz grapefruit juice
7-Up® soda

Instructions
Pour the vodka first, add grapefruit juice, and fill with about 6 ounces of 7-up or Sprite.

Serving
Highball Glass
****

Under Current recipe

Description
A delicious recipe for Under Current, with Absolut® Kurant vodka, Blue Curacao liqueur, sweet and sour mix, sugar syrup, Sprite® soda and Chambord® raspberry liqueur.

Ingredients
1 oz Absolut® Kurant vodka

1/2 oz Blue Curacao liqueur
1/2 oz sweet and sour mix
1/4 oz sugar syrup
1 splash Sprite® soda
1/4 oz Chambord® raspberry liqueur

Instructions
Mix everything except Chambord in a mixing tin, and pour into glass. Layer Chambord on top with a spoon.

Serving
Highball Glass
****

Under Kurant recipe

Description
A delicious recipe for Under Kurant, with Absolut® Kurant vodka, Blue Curacao liqueur, pineapple juice and Chambord® raspberry liqueur.

Ingredients
1 oz Absolut® Kurant vodka
1 1/2 oz Blue Curacao liqueur
1 oz pineapple juice
1/2 oz Chambord® raspberry liqueur

Instructions
Shake the absolut kurant, blue curacao, and pineapple juice with ice. Pour into a shot or low-ball glass, be sure and leave a bit of room to spare. Add just enough chambord to color the bottom of the glass.

Serving
Shot Glass
****

Vegas Lemon Drop Martini recipe

Description
A delicious recipe for Vegas Lemon Drop Martini, with Absolut® Citron

vodka, sugar and lemon.

Ingredients
1 1/2 oz Absolut® Citron vodka
1 tsp sugar
1/4 lemon

Instructions
Slice the 1/4 lemon into two seperate wedges. Place in a cocktail shaker half-filled with ice cubes. Pour the Absolut Citron into the shaker, and add one teaspoon of sugar. Shake vigorously. Strain into a sugar-rimmed cocktail glass. Garnish with a lemon twist, and serve.

Serving
Cocktail Glass
****

Very Berry Tonic recipe

Description
A delicious recipe for Very Berry Tonic, with Absolut® Kurant vodka, Chambord® raspberry liqueur and tonic water.

Ingredients
1 oz Absolut® Kurant vodka
1/2 oz Chambord® raspberry liqueur
tonic water

Instructions
Pour vodka and chambord into an ice-filled collins glass. Fill with tonic water, garnish with two fresh raspberries, and serve.

Serving
Collins Glass
****

Vicious Kiss recipe

Description
A delicious recipe for Vicious Kiss, with Absolut® Citron vodka, cherry juice and lime juice.

Ingredients
3 oz Absolut® Citron vodka
2 dashes cherry juice
2 splashes lime juice

Instructions
Pour into a cordial glass, stir gently, and serve.

Serving
Cordial Glass
****

Vodka Orange recipe

Description
A delicious recipe for Vodka Orange, with Absolut® vodka and orange juice.

Ingredients
1 part Absolut® vodka
2 parts orange juice

Instructions
Pour vodka over three or four ice cubes in a highball glass, and add fresh orange juice.

Serving
Highball Glass
****

Vodka Passion recipe

Description
A delicious recipe for Vodka Passion, with Absolut® Mandrin vodka and passion-fruit syrup.

Ingredients
1 part Absolut® Mandrin vodka
1 part passion-fruit syrup

Instructions
Mix both liquids over ice and strain into a shot glass.

Serving
Shot Glass
****

Waverunner recipe

Description
A delicious recipe for Waverunner, with Absolut® Citron vodka, sweet and sour mix, sugar, lemons, Chambord® raspberry liqueur and Champagne.

Ingredients
2 oz Absolut® Citron vodka
1 oz sweet and sour mix
2 tbsp sugar
2 lemons wedges
1/2 oz Chambord® raspberry liqueur
4 oz Champagne

Instructions
Shake all ingredients (except champagne) with ice. Strain into a sugar rimmed cocktail glass. Top with champagne. Squeeze and drop another wedge of lemon into the drink. (the other two should still be in the tin).

Serving
Cocktail Glass
****

Widow Maker recipe

Description
A delicious recipe for Widow Maker, with Absolut® vodka, Jagermeister® herbal liqueur, Kahlua® coffee liqueur and grenadine syrup.

Ingredients
1/2 oz Absolut® vodka
1/2 oz Jagermeister® herbal liqueur

1/2 oz Kahlua® coffee liqueur
2 drops grenadine syrup

Instructions
Fill an old-fashioned glass half full with ice. Add first three ingredients into the glass and sway lightly to mix them together. Add the 2 drops of grenadine for the red hour glass on the bottom of the widow maker spider.

Serving
Old-Fashioned Glass
****

Wiper Fluid recipe

Description
A delicious recipe for Wiper Fluid, with Hpnotiq® liqueur, pineapple juice, Stoli® Vanil vodka and Absolut® vodka.

Ingredients
1 oz Hpnotiq® liqueur
1 oz pineapple juice
1/2 oz Stoli® Vanil vodka
1/2 oz Absolut® vodka

Instructions
Combine all ingredients in a cocktail shaker with ice. Shake, strain into a cocktail glass, and serve.

Serving
Cocktail Glass
****

Wobbler recipe

Description
A delicious recipe for Wobbler, with Absolut® Kurant vodka, grape juice, Schweppes® Russian tonic water and grenadine syrup.

Ingredients
4 cl Absolut® Kurant vodka

grape juice
Schweppes® Russian tonic water
grenadine syrup

Instructions
Pour vodka into a glass one-quarter filled with ice. Fill until two-thirds full with grape juice, and fill completely with russian water. Add a touch of grenadine, and serve.

Serving
Highball Glass
****

Y2K Shot #2 recipe

Description
A delicious recipe for Y2K Shot #2, with Absolut® vodka, Midori® melon liqueur and Chambord® raspberry liqueur.

Ingredients
1 oz Absolut® vodka
1 oz Midori® melon liqueur
1 oz Chambord® raspberry liqueur

Instructions
Mix shot over ice in a mixing glass. Strain into shot glass.

Serving
Shot Glass
****

Yaka recipe

Description
A delicious recipe for Yaka, with Absolut® vodka, Everclear® alcohol, lemonade, lemons and water.

Ingredients
1 fifth Absolut® vodka
1 fifth Everclear® alcohol
1 bag lemonade

7 slices lemons
2 qt water

Instructions
Combine the water and lemonade mix, following the directions on the lemonade mix. Add everclear and absolut vodka. Then add the lemon slices and shake to mix. Serve cold.

Serving
Pitcher
****

Zadarade recipe

Description
A delicious recipe for Zadarade, with Absolut® Mandrin vodka, triple sec, sweet and sour mix, cranberry juice, pineapple juice, lemon-lime soda and ice cubes.

Ingredients
1 oz Absolut® Mandrin vodka
1 oz triple sec
1 oz sweet and sour mix
1 splash cranberry juice
1 splash pineapple juice
1 splash lemon-lime soda
ice cubes

Instructions
Fill glass with ice cubes. Add absolut mandrin, triple sec, and sour mix. Add a splash of cranberry juice, and pineapple. Shake, and top with a splash of lemon-lime soda.

Serving
Collins Glass
****

Zool recipe

Description
A delicious recipe for Zool, with peach schnapps, Absolut® vodka and

amaretto almond liqueur.

Ingredients
1 oz peach schnapps
1 oz Absolut® vodka
1 oz amaretto almond liqueur

Instructions
Pour peach schnapps into a shot glass, and add vodka. Add amaretto until vodka turns to a light brown, and serve.

Serving
Shot Glass
****

Made in the USA
Las Vegas, NV
23 May 2024